Thomas K. Johnson

Humanitarian Islam, Evangelical Christianity, and the Clash of Civilizations

To the cover motif: Sri Ayati's Legacy depicts a slain Catholic freedom fighter, whose lifeless body lies cradled in the arms of Indonesia's first president, Soekarno. The painting vividly illustrates why the world's largest Muslim-majority nation and democracy was established as a multi-religious/pluralistic state, with a constitutional guarantee of equal rights for all its citizens, and has been adopted by Gerakan Pemuda Ansor as a symbol of the Humanitarian Islam movement. (https://libforall.org/what-we-do/)

World of Theology Series

Published by the Theological Commission of the World Evangelical Alliance

Volume 20

Thomas K. Johnson

Humanitarian Islam, Evangelical Christianity, and the Clash of Civilizations:

A New Partnership for Peace and Religious Freedom

WIPF & STOCK · Eugene, Oregon

Wipf and Stock Publishers
199 W 8th Ave, Suite 3
Eugene, OR 97401

Humanitarian Islam, Evangelical Christianity, and the Clash of Civilizations:
A New Partnership for Peace and Religious Freedom
By Johnson, Thomas K.
Copyright © 2021 Verlag für Kultur und Wissenschaft Culture and Science Publ. All rights reserved.
Softcover ISBN-13: 978-1-6667-0439-6
Hardcover ISBN-13: 978-1-6667-0440-2
Publication date 3/4/2021
Previously published by Verlag für Kultur und Wissenschaft Culture and Science Publ., 2021

Contents

Death When Religions Collide[1]

In spring 2007, I was scheduled to teach a theology class for a low-visibility Evangelical seminary in Turkey. I had just received a list of students. On April 19, 2007, I opened my email and felt as if I had been kicked in the stomach. Terrorists had slit the throat of one of our seminary students; two other people had suffered similar fates. Three men were dead: two Turkish converts from Islam to Christianity, one German missionary. Two wives were suddenly widows; four young children lost their fathers. They died because they were Christians; their place of death was a Bible publishing house in Malatya, Turkey. The motives of their murderers were a sinister mix of nationalist ideology and the desire to enforce an inhumane version of sharia, or Muslim law. A type of Turkish nationalism says that Christians may no longer be good Turks, especially if they have converted from Islam. It was a terrible mess of religious and political motives. Bad ideas had led to disaster.[2]

I soon learned that most Muslims are sickened to see their religion used to justify violence. The average Muslim is neither a terrorist nor a murderer. However, the three murders in Malatya took their place in a long line of war, death, and destruction centered in Turkey and the broader Middle East and in which the warring parties were sometimes described as Islam versus Christianity and sometimes as Islam versus the West. One historian entitled a chapter "Islam Takes Christendom by Storm: The Battle of Yarmuk, 636" at the outset of 300 pages on *Fourteen Centuries of War between Islam and the West*.[3] In the fateful event of 636 CE, two Christian armies, representing the Byzantine Empire and the Kingdom of Ghassan, faced a Muslim army sent by the Rashidun Caliphate. The death toll reached the tens of thousands during the battle east of the Sea of Galilee, today the borderlands of Israel, Jordan, and Syria.[4] The Muslim victory was

---

[1] *The opinions expressed in this report are those of Dr. Johnson. They are offered for discussion and study by the World Evangelical Alliance.*

[2] For more on this tragedy, see "Commemorations of the 10th Anniversary of the Martyrs of Malatya," *Bonn Profiles* 11/2017, available here: https://www.bucer.de/ressource/details/bonner-querschnitte-112017-ausgabe-472-eng.html.

[3] Raymond Ibrahim, *Sword and Scimitar: Fourteen Centuries of War between Islam and the West* (Hachette Books: Kindle Edition, 2018).

[4] Philip Jenkins notes, "The battle of Yarmuk in 636, which gave the Muslims control of Syria, was one of the great military massacres of antiquity, costing the lives of perhaps fifty thousand soldiers of the Christian Byzantine Empire." *The Lost History of Christianity* (Harper One: Kindle Edition, 2009), 101.

a milestone in their conquest of the Levant and north Africa from the 630s to the 730s, which had long been the center from which Christianity had extended east into Asia, south into Africa, and north toward Europe. In 2007, many in the Middle East perceived the murder of our seminary student as the continuation of the wars started 1,400 years before.

The end of the era of jihads and crusades is difficult to define. Did the crusades end with the fall of Acre in 1291, as Western Christians have usually claimed?[5] Or did this era continue till the fall of Constantinople in 1453? Till the battle of Vienna in 1683? Till the destruction of the Ottoman Caliphate in 1924? Or has this era never ended? In the twenty-first century, addressing the present situation and speaking in the present tense, Princeton University professor Bernard Lewis noted, "The Crusades figure very prominently in modern Middle Eastern consciousness and discourse."[6]

These wars have continuing significance, even if the West no longer calls itself Christian and if Christians in the West have largely forgotten this history. After the end of the Ottoman Empire in 1922, Islam did not have a caliphate, and therefore Islam did not appear to be a global political force. In the West it seemed justified to forget that wars with Islam once played a defining role in our history. Those who became Muslim extremists did not forget. "When the Islamic State declares that 'American blood is best, and we will taste it soon,' or 'We love death as you love life,' or 'We will conquer your Rome, break your crosses, and enslave your women,' virtually no one in the West understands that they are quoting the verbatim words — and placing themselves within the footsteps — of their jihadi forbears as recounted in the preceding history."[7] Though one might not know the ideology of the murderers in Turkey in detail, Muslim extremists of the twenty-first century are continuing the wars started in the 630s.[8]

---

[5]   For an overview, dating, and assessment of the crusades from a standard Western Christian perspective, see Kenneth Scott Latourette, *A History of Christianity: Vol. 1, Beginnings to 1500* (Harper & Row, 1975), 408-415. "Here was an effort to achieve the kingdom of God on earth by the methods of the world which the New Testament declares to be at enmity with the Gospel" (p. 414).

[6]   Bernard Lewis, *The Crisis of Islam: Holy War and Unholy Terror* (New York: Random House, 2003), 47.

[7]   Ibrahim, 296.

[8]   Bernard Lewis comments, "Much of the anger in the Islamic world is directed against the Westerner, seen as the ancient and immemorial enemy of Islam since the first clashes between the Muslim caliphs and the Christian emperors, and against the Westernizer, seen as a tool or accomplice of the West and as a traitor to his own faith and people" (p. 132). To cite Lewis again, "For them [Muslim fundamentalists] the remedy is a return to true Islam, including the abolition of all the laws and other social borrowings from the West and the restoration of the

During the last decade, diplomats, senior religious leaders, parliamen-tarians, and retired heads of state have shared their concern since 2001 that a new world war could break out between Islam and the West. In small gatherings we have all worried that an undeclared and undefined world war was already starting; many wondered if Samuel Huntington might be right regarding a "Clash of Civilizations," though everyone hoped he was wrong.[9] This formed the background for the 2019 Human Fraternity Docu-ment signed by Pope Francis and the Grand Imam of Al-Azhar, assessed below. That text described "what might be referred to as signs of a 'third world war being fought piecemeal'. In several parts of the world and in many tragic circumstances these signs have begun to be painfully appar-ent, as in those situations where the precise number of victims, widows and orphans is unknown." Such concerns provide context for the murder of my future seminary student: was his death one of a thousand on the way to a world war?[10]

Shari'a as the effective law of the land. From their point of view, the ultimate struggle is not against the Western intruder but against the Westernizing traitor at home" (p. 134).

[9]   In his 1993 essay "The Clash of Civilizations?" Huntington argued, "Conflict be-tween civilizations will be the latest phase of the evolution of conflict in the mod-ern world" (p. 1). "Civilizations are differentiated from each other by history, lan-guage, culture, tradition, and most important, religion" (p. 4). "This centuries-old military interaction between the West and Islam is unlikely to decline" (p. 9). "On both sides the interaction between Islam and the West is seen as a clash of civili-zations" (p. 10). *Foreign Affairs* Vol. 72, No. 3 (Summer, 1993), 22-49. This essay, along with several critical responses, was republished as a book, *The Clash of Civili-zations? The Debate* (New York: Foreign Affairs, 1966). Page numbers are from the second publication. One of the better criticisms of Huntington's perspective claimed that he overemphasized political culture and underemphasized sexuality. Ronald Inglehart and Pippa Norris, "The True Clash of Civilizations," *Foreign Policy*, November 4, 2009; available here: https://www.bucer.de/ressource/details/bon ner-querschnitte-112017-ausgabe-472-eng.html.

[10] In his 1996 book, Huntington expanded and perhaps modified his explanation of the clash between Islam and the West. "The causes of this ongoing pattern of con-flict lie not in transitory phenomena such as twelfth-century Christian passion or twentieth-century Muslim fundamentalism. They flow from the nature of the two religions and the civilizations based on them. Conflict was, on the one hand, a product of difference, particularly the Muslim concept of Islam as a way of life transcending and uniting religion and politics versus the Western Christian con-cept of the separate realms of God and Caesar. The conflict also stemmed, how-ever, from their similarities. Both are monotheistic religions, which, unlike poly-theistic ones, cannot easily assimilate additional deities, and which see the world in dualistic, us-and-them terms. Both are universalistic, claiming to be the one true faith to which all humans can adhere. Both are missionary religions believing

Students of history know that Malatya, where our student was killed, is in Eastern Anatolia. Eastern Anatolia was called Western Armenia until the Ottoman Empire outlawed the word "Armenia" to refer to this region in 1880. This was the center of the Armenian genocide. Ottoman religious authorities declared a jihad against the Christian minorities within their empire, beginning on April 24, 1915. This came after the Ottoman Empire under the leadership of the "Young Turks," who had just seized power, entered World War I on the side of Germany and the Austro-Hungarian Empire. The jihad cost the lives of some 1.5 million Armenian Christians, along with an estimated 300,000 Greek-speaking Christians and 300,000 Aramaic-speaking Christians. It was part of a broader pattern within the Muslim world. Phillip Jenkins writes, "From the First World War onward, Christian communities were systematically eliminated across the Muslim world, and the Armenian horrors of 1915 are only the most glaring of a series of such atrocities that reached their peak between 1915 and 1925. Although these instances of massacre and persecution have no historical resonance for most Westerners today, they count among the worst examples of their kind."[11]

A solution to the deaths at the point where Islam and Christianity collide should involve theological development and interfaith cooperation. At times, both religions included notions of religiously defined nations within their ethics; this contributed to involving religions in the conflicts among nations. Such religious doctrines also weakened religious resistance to atrocities within religiously defined nations. An ideal theological development would place Islam and Christianity on the same side, outside and above the normal conflicts among nations, offering a universal ethical compass for all. Such a radical step is, I believe, possible via a partnership between Evangelical Christianity and Humanitarian Islam.

---

that their adherents have an obligation to convert nonbelievers to that one true faith. From its origins Islam expanded by conquest and when the opportunity existed Christianity did also." Samuel P. Huntington, *The Clash of Civilizations and the Remaking of World Order* (New York: Simon & Schuster, 1996), 210, 211.

[11]   Jenkins, *Lost History*, 156.

Partial Muslim Responses to Religious Violence

In recent years, many Muslim theologians have been working to convince extremists to turn from violence while explaining to the watching world why violence does not represent Islam. Such Muslim theologians perceive their urgent intellectual debt, knowing their religious community and the rest of the world need a well-articulated perspective on Islam that opposes violence. Since there existed no statement with wide public support from Muslim religious officials rejecting the violent Islamist agenda, the rest of the world was rightfully asking if Muslim religious authorities were indifferent to the behavior of violent Muslims who claim religious motivation, whether they are a local group of thugs (such as in Turkey), ISIS, Al-Qaeda, Boko Haram, or others.[12]

The notoriety gained by ISIS, especially by their proclamation of themselves as the Caliphate in 2014, increased the urgency felt by Muslim intellectuals who oppose extremism. Three prominent responses have been: 1) the "Open Letter to Dr. Ibrahim Awwad Al-Badri, alias 'Abu Bakr Al-Baghdadi,' and to the fighters and followers of the self-declared 'Islamic State'" published by 126 Sunni leaders in September 2014; 2) the Marrakesh Declaration of 2016; and 3) the 2019 Human Fraternity Document (HFD) signed in Abu Dhabi by Pope Francis and the Grand Imam of Al-Azhar, mentioned above.[13]

These documents directly confront and condemn violence in the name of Islam; were these principles followed, our world would be safer.

---

[12] Abdurrahman Wahid, one-time president of Indonesia, began to address this problem earlier than some other governmental leaders. See his "Right Islam vs. Wrong Islam: Muslims and Non-Muslims Must Unite to Defeat the Wahhabi Ideology," *The Wall Street Journal*, 30 December 2005, available here: https://www.wsj.com/articles/SB113590649048834335. Confirmed 1 April 2020. See also James M. Dorsey, "Reforming the Faith: Indonesia's Battle for the Soul of Islam," *Horizons: Journal of International Relations and Sustainable Development* Winter 2019 No. 13, 150-171, available here: https://www.cirsd.org/files/000/000/006/37/b645306043a5a372d10f9cdc65146d3fccc9e778.pdf.

[13] Muslim leaders from around the world have openly condemned violence committed in the name of Islam on many occasions in recent years, but their condemnations have not been so widely reported in the media as the more prominent examples mentioned here. The Islamic Networks Group, based in California, maintains a list of Muslim denunciations of violence committed in the name of Islam. See https://ing.org/global-condemnations-of-isis-isil/.

However, these recent Muslim statements perpetuate some convictions that undermine their potential to reduce tragedies. For example, the Open Letter of 2014 (paragraph 22) affirms the obligation of Muslims to form a new caliphate, though rejecting ISIS's use of morally repugnant means to establish a caliphate. The desire to restore a caliphate is a central cause of conflicts among Muslims as well as between Islam and other cultures; this problem is perpetuated by the Open Letter. Moreover, the moral argumentation used to condemn the atrocities committed by ISIS is predominantly an exegesis of the contents of Islam, without extensive reference to standards of behavior that are understandable by people of other religions or no religion. Even if not intentional, this approach communicates that these spokesmen had not appreciated the need of the Muslim community to give a moral account to humanity. A moral account to humanity must refer to standards known to all of humanity, not only standards known to Muslims, unless they wish to communicate that one has to be a Muslim to distinguish between right and wrong.

Likewise, the Marrakesh Declaration of 2016, though rejecting violence in the name of Islam and calling for the development of a Muslim doctrine of citizenship that applies to people of other religions, clearly affirms the notion of "Muslim countries." In a Muslim country as defined by the declaration, minorities may be tolerated, and citizenship may increase their level of toleration, but non-Muslims will always be regarded and treated as something less than full stakeholders. It seems as if the Marrakesh doctrine of a Muslim country is a smaller version of the Muslim doctrine of which the Caliphate is the larger version. The Marrakesh Declaration lacks a sense that justice requires the equal treatment of individuals and communities who adhere to various religions in such a manner that a country should no longer be officially described as a Muslim country. The Marrakesh Declaration does not affirm comprehensive freedom of religion; despite its rejection of religiously motivated violence, it affirms one of the key ideas that leads to religiously motivated violence and war, to repeat, the doctrine of a religiously defined country. The murderers of our seminary student thought Turkey should be a Muslim country, and Boko Haram is using atrocities to turn parts of Nigeria into a Muslim state.[14]

---

[14] The best alternative to a religiously defined nation is not secularism. The best alternative is a multi-religious state that allows and expects multiple religions to be active within a nation with equivalent rights, while also recognizing the full rights of people without a defined religion. Multiple religions can even contribute to culture and politics within the same country in a peaceful and constructive manner, if the roles of religions in society are configured wisely.

The previously mentioned Human Fraternity Document of 2019 (HFD) blends important themes in Roman Catholic and Sunni Muslim ethical teaching in a manner that is designed to be understood by followers of either religion or of no religion. It begins to address the problems related to minority religions and citizenship which were identified in the Marrakesh Declaration. The HFD could be a valuable tool for moral instruction in some circumstances; it has the added value of clarifying international and interfaith ethical standards for many areas of public life, though some will wonder if this text implies an undue ultimate equivalence of religious beliefs.[15] Despite these significant steps forward, the HFD does not explicitly address the problem of the religiously defined state, whether one has a Christian country or a Muslim country in view. By ignoring this topic, the text may unintentionally perpetuate second-class citizenship for adherents of minority religions. And the HFD does not address the issue of how to treat people who convert from one religion to another. The reality of people changing religions, along with the philosophical and emotional discussions of religions that surround such conversions, is explosive. Seemingly as a dimension of globalization, people from around the world are changing their religious affiliations; there is no way to stop such conversions short of extreme levels of censorship and force. As the story from Turkey illustrates, such conversions are flashpoints for extremism in any social context in which religious identity, and especially a change of religious identity, can exclude people from being perceived as full and proper citizens. The closest the HFD comes to addressing violence related to conversions is the claim that "the fact that people are forced to adhere to a certain religion or culture must be rejected." A convincing statement on religiously motivated violence must explain a position on conversion between religions that is convincing to people of all religions or no religion.

Some recent Muslim statements on public life, such as those just discussed, make passing reference to the 1948 United Nations' Universal Declaration of Human Rights (UDHR). However, UDHR article 18, which is painfully explicit about the freedom to convert to a different religion, is seldom quoted. It states, "Everyone has the right to freedom of thought, conscience and religion; this right includes freedom to change his religion

---

[15] For example, the HFD claims, "The pluralism and the diversity of religions, colour, sex, race and language are willed by God in His wisdom, through which He created human beings." Many Christians hold exclusive truth claims that would make them hesitate to say without qualification that "God willed the diversity of religions." Recognition of the similarities of ethical teaching across faith traditions should be balanced by a recognition of the ultimate incompatibility of some claims of those traditions.

or belief, and freedom, either alone or in community with others and in public or private, to manifest his religion or belief in teaching, practice, worship and observance." If UDHR 18 were fully understood, affirmed, and practiced, it would not only end the persecution of converts; it would also mean the gradual end of the religious definition of countries (whether Muslim, Christian, Hindu, or Buddhist). No country that consistently protects the freedom to change religions, including freedom to develop the institutions of newly adopted religions, can consistently affirm its long-term identity as a state belonging to one religion.

A Comprehensive Muslim Solution to Religious Violence

One Muslim movement addressing religious extremism is qualitatively different from most such efforts; the difference is immediately evident not only by the movement's robust affirmation of the UDHR (including article 18), but also by the rejection of the notion of a Muslim country or caliphate. Their representatives go far beyond saying that Muslims should not murder people who convert to another religion. They address foundational religious doctrines and contextualize their theory of ethics in relation to religiously pluralistic societies, in view of the history of religiously motivated conflict. This movement, with the advantage of long historical roots in Indonesia, has been articulated by official representatives of the massive Muslim organization Nahdlatul Ulama (NU). Their perspective is now called "Humanitarian Islam" and has spawned many publications in English for the international community, especially since ISIS declared its caliphate in 2014.

A careful examination of the ethics of Humanitarian Islam finds that Muslims of this type support religious freedom and human rights for Christians and people of other faiths. But this ethic goes much farther. Though presented as a Muslim alternative to extremist violence, Humanitarian Islam contains a serious assessment of universal moral norms, the relation between faith and reason, fundamental human goods, the laws (both civil and religious) needed to protect those human goods, and the role of religions in societies.[16] A comparison of Humanitarian Muslim philosophy and ethics with Christian ethics and philosophy of law reveals that, amidst the great global threats, Christians and Humanitarian Muslims are ideological allies and should treat each other as such. There are major theological differences between Christians and Muslims, such as the Christian knowledge of God as a Trinity, that may never be resolved, but the level of agreement in the spheres of ethics and law calls for global cooperation in the public square. Rather than being in opposing armies in a potential clash of civilizations, Evangelical Christians and Humanitarian Muslims should protect each other's religious communities while articulating and embodying a global moral compass.

---

[16] I am using the term "human goods" in a specialized manner. In this text it refers to the several values, institutions, and practices that promote flourishing for individuals and communities.

Humanitarian Islam: A New Muslim Orthodoxy

Within the spectrum of varieties of Islam, the Humanitarians represent the opposite end from the violent extremists. They present themselves as fully orthodox Muslims, not secularized half-Muslims. Precisely as such, they fully endorse classical human rights, religious freedom for other religions, and constitutional democracy, while openly naming and repudiating "obsolete and problematic tenets" of Muslim orthodoxy which, they claim, have been misused to promote extremism.[17]

To grasp the Humanitarians' doctrinal development, one should start with their reason for reforming or re-contextualizing Muslim orthodoxy. Humanitarian Islam believes that Islamic extremists — from ISIS to the Wahhabis of Saudi Arabia — have been misusing Islam for their own purposes and that this misuse of religion has been supported by versions of Muslim doctrine which were contextualized many centuries ago in a radically different situation. In the *Declaration on Humanitarian Islam* (May 2017) they write, "The Islamic world is in the midst of a rapidly metastasizing crisis, with no apparent sign of remission. Among the most obvious manifestations of this crisis are the brutal conflicts now raging across a huge swath of territory inhabited by Muslims, from Africa and the Middle East to the borders of India; rampant social turbulence throughout the Islamic world; the unchecked spread of religious extremism and terror; and a rising tide of Islamophobia among non-Muslim populations, in direct response to these developments" (para 25).[18] They add, "the crisis that

---

[17] For example, in February 2019, NU leaders decreed that the term "infidel" may no longer be used to describe people who are not Muslims, suggesting that the term "citizen" be used as a replacement. For the political context, see "NU calls for end to word 'infidels' to describe non-Muslims," *Jakarta Post,* March 1, 2019, available here: https://www.thejakartapost.com/news/2019/03/01/nu-calls-for-end-to-word-infidels-to-describe-non-muslims.html. Confirmed 1 April 2020. The decree itself is found here: https://www.baytarrahmah.org/media/2019/2019-Munas_Findings-of-Bahtsul-Masa%E2%80%99il-Maudluiyyah.pdf. An explanation of the significance of this action is found here: https://baytarrahmah.org/2019_10_16_world-first-nahdlatul-ulama-abolishes-the-legal-category-of-infidel-within-islamic-law/.

[18] "Gerakan Pemuda Ansor Declaration on Humanitarian Islam: Towards the Recontextualization of Islamic Teachings for the Sake of World Peace and Harmony Between Civilizations" (Jombang, East Java, Indonesia: Bayt ar-Rahmah, 2017), available here: https://www.baytarrahmah.org/media/2017/Gerakan-Pemuda-

engulfs the Islamic world is not limited to armed conflicts raging in various and sundry regions" (para 27). "Various actors — including but not limited to Iran, Saudi Arabia, ISIS, al-Qaeda, Hezbollah, Qatar, the Muslim Brotherhood, the Taliban and Pakistan — cynically manipulate religious sentiment in their struggle to maintain or acquire political, economic and military power, and to destroy their enemies. They do so by drawing upon key elements of classical Islamic law (*fiqh*), to which they ascribe divine authority, in order to mobilize support for their worldly goals" (para 28). Extremists manipulate religion to gain power by means of ascribing divine authority to a distinctive interpretation of Islamic law which the extremists describe as orthodox.

This crisis of the Islamic world, as the Humanitarians see it, is not limited to the conflicts among Muslims. It includes religious terrorism practiced against non-Muslims, which promotes Islamophobia and the resulting attacks on Islam. They use the term "weaponization of Islam" to describe the way in which particular themes of Muslim doctrine, especially certain elements in classical Islamic law, have become a tool of war. For example, the declaration of a Caliphate was used by ISIS to mobilize support for their attacks on Muslims who did not support ISIS and to mobilize support for attacks on people of other religions. In response, people from various countries began to describe Islam or all Muslim people as enemies, using religion, especially the fear of Islam, as a weapon to increase their power in their own countries.

According to Ansor Chairman H. Yaqut Qoumas, "No progress can be made towards neutralizing a threat, unless it is understood and identified. It is false and counterproductive to claim that the actions of al-Qaeda, ISIS, Boko Haram and other such groups have nothing to do with Islam, or merely represent a perversion of Islamic teachings. They are, in fact, outgrowths of Wahhabism and other fundamentalist streams of Sunni Islam." He continues, "Muslims face a choice between starkly different visions of the future. Will they strive to recreate the long-lost ideal of religious, political and territorial unity beneath the banner of a Caliphate ... ? Or will they strive to develop a new religious sensibility that reflects the actual circumstances of our modern civilization, and contributes to the

---

Ansor_Declaration-on-Humanitarian-Islam.pdf. Confirmed 1 April 2020. For context, see the Bayt ar-Rahmah political communiqué of May 22, 2017, available here: https://baytarrahmah.org/2017_05_22_ansor-declaration-on-humanitarian-islam/.

emergence of a truly just and harmonious world order, founded upon respect for the equal dignity and rights of every human being?"[19]

Therefore, the *Declaration on Humanitarian Islam* says, "If Muslims do not
address the key tenets of Islamic orthodoxy that authorize and explicitly
enjoin such violence, anyone — at any time — may harness the orthodox
teachings of Islam to defy what they claim to be the illegitimate laws and
authority of an infidel state and butcher their fellow citizens, regardless of
whether they live in the Islamic world or the West. This is the bloody
thread that links so many current events, from Egypt, Syria and Yemen to
the streets of Mumbai, Jakarta, Berlin, Nice, Stockholm and Westminster"
(para 13). Therefore, they are developing a new Islamic orthodoxy, a "new
religious sensibility," that addresses the problematic tenets of medieval Islamic teaching which extremists claim are orthodox.

Precisely as Muslims, the Humanitarians claim that the extremists do
not reflect Islam at its best. The core of their argument is that Islam has a
tradition of developing the application of Muslim ethics and law by means
of interaction with changing cultures but that this process stopped several
centuries ago; this has left many Muslims bound to an ossified and conflict-
producing version of sharia that is not tenable in a global, pluralistic society. In contrast, truly orthodox Islam contains within itself its own proper
theological and legal method for developing its teaching; this method
leads to a humanitarian, pro-democracy position, including promoting religious freedom for all, signaling the end of religiously defined countries.
Humanitarian Islam seeks to reactivate this authentically Muslim theological method to develop a truly new and yet more fully orthodox Islam, dis-
placing the Wahhabi Islam that is fueling many conflicts and a global clash
of civilizations.

In their words, "As the majority of '*ulamā*' [Muslim scholars] have traditionally recognized, Islamic orthodoxy consists of both transcendent
(i.e., immutable) elements (*thawābit*) and contingent responses to historical reality (*mutaghayyirāt*), which may be adapted to address and reflect
the ever-changing circumstances of life" (*Nusantara Manifesto* para 102).
"Islamic orthodoxy contains internal mechanisms, including the science
of *uṣūl al-fiqh* — the methodology of independent legal reasoning employed
to create Islamic law, or *fiqh* (often conflated with *sharīʿah*) — that allow
Muslim scholars to adjust the temporal elements of religious orthodoxy in
response to the ever-changing circumstances of life. These internal mechanisms entail a process of independent legal reasoning known as *ijtihād*,
which fell into disuse among Sunni Muslim scholars approximately five

---

[19] As quoted in the Bayt ar-Rahmah political communiqué of May 22, 2017.

centuries ago" (*Nusantara Manifesto* para 106). As they see it, for 500 years the proper Muslim theological method, the "internal mechanism" for the unfolding of Muslim orthodoxy, has not been properly implemented, leading to the debacle of the role of Islam on the global stage. This situation leaves their thought leaders with a lot of unfinished homework.

To quote their manifesto:

> "To date, there has been no systematic effort by Muslim authorities to adapt the temporal elements — i.e., the historically-determined 'operational values' — of Islamic orthodoxy to reflect and address these changes. The current crisis of the Muslim world may be largely attributed to this failure, as evidenced by extremist efforts to reestablish an Islamic Caliphate; abolish nation states; reject laws derived from modern political processes; and revivify obsolete elements of *fiqh* (which they invariably conflate with *sharī'ah*), such as offensive *jihād*, slavery, the subordination of infidels, stoning adulterers, executing homosexuals and amputating the hands of thieves" (*Nusantara Manifesto* para 109).

Theological Method

Six themes characterize the theological method used by Humanitarian Islam in its systematic effort to define a new Islamic ethics and theory of law.

1. Eternal norms versus contingent norms

Humanitarian Muslims have clarified the hermeneutic they use to work with classical Muslim texts and principles. In the *Declaration on Humanitarian Islam* they write, "Religious norms may be universal and unchanging — e.g., the imperative that one strive to attain moral and spiritual perfection — or they may be 'contingent,' if they address a specific issue that arises within the ever-changing circumstances of time and place. As reality changes, contingent — as opposed to universal — religious norms should also change to reflect the constantly shifting circumstances of life on earth" (paras 3 and 4). The contrast between eternal norms and contingent norms is the key to their hermeneutic.

The crisis of Islam arises, they claim, from taking contingent norms from previous centuries, whether it is the seventh century or the Middle Ages, and then applying them in the twenty-first century as if they are eternal, unchanging norms. This leads to a horrendous misperception of Islamic religious rules, both by Islamist extremists and by the enemies of Islam. "Horrors of the past such as slavery, crucifixion and the public execution of alleged homosexuals, adulterers, infidels, apostates and magicians are resurrected, reinstituted as valid components of an Islamic social order and broadcast to a disgusted global audience" (*Nusantara Manifesto* para 80). Regardless of how one evaluates past criminal law requiring, for example, amputation as punishment for theft, exactly how theft should be punished is not an eternal norm. Different punishments are suitable today. This is their hermeneutic at work.

The eternal norms cited by Humanitarian Islam are general principles of morally sensitive behavior. For example, they emphasize the need "to revitalize the understanding and practice of religion as *raḥmah* (universal love and compassion)" in contrast with hatred and violence (*Manifesto* para 7). They continue, "Noble behavior entails acting with compassion and treating others with respect" (para 61). As a dimension of respect for others, they repeatedly mention the UDHR (for example, para 132).

The way in which the Muslim community should recognize and re-contextualize eternal norms into religious norms suitable for our era has to do with attaining defined fundamental human goods which are central components of human flourishing. "The purpose of religious norms (*maqasid al-shari'ah*) is to ensure the spiritual and material well-being of humanity" (*Declaration* para 1). They add, "The authoritative Sunni jurists, Imam al-Ghazali and Imam al-Shatibi, identified five primary components of *maqasid al-shari'ah*, viz., the preservation of faith, life, progeny, reason and property" (para 2). This strikingly teleological way of reasoning about religious and civil norms also appears within Christian ethics, meriting further discussion below. Properly formulated contingent norms must be articulated by religious authorities in a manner that promotes and protects human flourishing and especially these five defined primary human goods.[20]

2. A transcendental definition of sharia

The definition of "sharia" (with different spellings in various languages) is important when one considers the varieties of Islam. Humanitarian Islam is distinguished from some other types of Islam by the way it applies the term "sharia" to eternal norms, not to specific, contingent civil laws or criminal punishments.

Because of the complex origin of sharia in the Koran, in the early Muslim tradition, and in the interpretations of classical Muslim theology, sharia does not have an historically given source or definition found in one text. Some describe it as an orientation or a set of expectations, not a precise code of laws as found in modern jurisprudence; nor should one compare sharia too closely with a particular biblical text, such as the Ten Commandments, which is often called "the law" in Christian ethics. Christine Schirrmacher notes the problem within Sunni Islam of the existence of "six extensive collections by various authors taken to be authoritative and containing tens of thousands of individual texts on numerous topics.

---

[20]   In some Muslim discussions, the terminology of "five basic human needs" is used. For example, Mujiburrahman writes, "One of the examples of how Islam pays serious attention to human dignity is manifest in the principle of Islamic law known as the protection of five basic human needs (*daruriyyat*), namely (1) the protection of self (*hifz al-nafs*) from any violation; (2) the protection of religion (*hifz al-diri*) from any enforced conversion; (3) the protection of family and next generation (*hifz al-nasl*); (4) the protection of personal property (*hifz al-mal*); and (5) the protection of profession or intellect (*hifz al-aql*)." Mujiburrahman, "Islam and Politics in Indonesia: the Political Thought of Abdurrahman Wahid," *Islam and Christian–Muslim Relations*, Vol. 10, No. 3, 1999; 342.

These, in turn, have differences among themselves and even indicate contradictory differences with respect to legal statements."[21]

Despite the complicated textual basis of sharia, there is within some varieties of Islam a perception of considerable unity of content. It is this view of sharia which Humanitarian Islam brings under systematic critique. This perceived unity is great enough that several countries have attempted to fully implement a specific set of laws that they call "the sharia," even if the historical claim that this is the true sharia is questionable. For example, Sudan, Pakistan, Libya, parts of Nigeria, the Aceh province of Indonesia, some regions in the Philippines, and Yemen have, in the twentieth or twenty-first century, implemented sharia law to strictly enforce such matters as women's dress, punishment for blasphemy or apostasy, corporal punishment, stoning for adultery, and even cutting off limbs.[22]

Humanitarian Islam decries this practice as the false application of contingent religious norms from a previous era to the current situation. Instead, the term "sharia," which the Humanitarians use sparingly, is applied to eternal principles that exist outside time and space. They see sharia as transcendent moral values leading to God (and protecting creation) that must be newly applied in every situation, not as specific laws that can be enforced by a police officer. The *Nusantara Manifesto* (2018) included an essay by Kyai Haji Abdurrahman Wahid (1940–2009), President of Indonesia from 1999 to 2001, called "God Needs No Defense," as an official appendix. Wahid wrote, "In its original Qur'anic sense, the word shari'a refers to 'the way,' the path to God, and not to formally codified Islamic law, which only emerged in the centuries following Muhammad's death." Wahid continued, "Shari'a, properly understood, expresses and embodies perennial values. Islamic law, on the other hand, is the product of *ijtihad* (interpretation) which depends on circumstances (*al-hukm yadur ma'a al-'illah wujudan wa 'adaman*) and needs to be continuously reviewed in accordance with ever-changing circumstances, to prevent Islamic law from becoming out of date, rigid and non-correlative — not only with Muslims' contemporary lives and conditions, but also with the underlying perennial values of shari'a itself."[23] In other words, "the way" cannot merely copy a law code

---

[21]   Christine Schirrmacher, *The Sharia: Law and Order in Islam*, trans. Richard McClary, ed. Thomas K. Johnson (Bonn: World Evangelical Alliance, 2013), 17; online here: https://iirf.eu/journal-books/global-issues-series/the-sharia-law-and-order-in-islam.

[22]   Schirrmacher, *The Sharia*, 24.

[23]   These and subsequent quotations of President Wahid are taken from pages 30 to 32 of the *Nusantara Manifesto*.

from a previous era; perennial and eternal values have to be applied in every generation, for which a clear theological and legal method is needed.

Wahid assumed that in some instances, religious law as taught today, based on contingent interpretations from a previous era, would contradict a proper contingent interpretation or application of the perennial values of the eternal, higher sharia to our era. For example, anti-blasphemy or anti-apostasy laws, which may have been proper applications of the eternal sharia in a previous socio-political situation, might themselves become blasphemous in our era because they attempt to defend God in ways that are inappropriate in a multi-religious society.

Wahid argued that punishment for apostasy (which intends to defend God) dated back to a time "when apostasy generally coincided with desertion from the Caliph's army and/or rejection of his authority, and thus constituted treason or rebellion." Accordingly, the punishment was contingent on a particular historical context and should not be applied to all contexts.

As used by Humanitarian Islam, the sharia is a transcendent set of principles that must be discerned in a process of moral reflection. Such principles can become contemporary religious norms when articulated by the scholars representing a religious community; these principles are designed to protect and promote the primary human goods of life, faith, progeny, reason, and property, in a particular time and place.[24]

Such a definition of sharia, if followed by the global Muslim movement, would undermine most reasons for Islamophobia, since it would shift the discussion of the religious ethics of public life away from, for example, the proper way to execute blasphemers and toward a principled discussion of what human goods are primary and what types of religious and civil laws would protect those human goods. People from different religious communities and cultures might have different opinions, but the discussion of human goods and the proper ways to protect human flourishing would constitute civil public discourse, not an endless war.

---

[24]   On the varieties of understandings of sharia in Indonesia, Bernard Adeney-Risakotta commented, "In Indonesia the concern with morality is not confined to the private sphere. Public law is meant to incorporate morality and guide the society toward goodness. Muslims view Sharia (the way of God) as absolute truth which must be obeyed. However, there are great differences in Muslim interpretations of how 'the way of God' should be applied in society. For example, some Muslims view the essence of Sharia as justice, peace, human rights, and responsibilities which can be formulated differently in different places and times. Others understand Sharia as an ancient law code that grew up in the centuries after prophet, detailing dress for women and specific punishments for various crimes." *Living in a Sacred Cosmos: Indonesia and the Future of Islam* (Yale University, 2018), 67.

3. Humanitarian Islam and Nusantara civilization

Humanitarian Islam claims that important moral and political principles that have long existed in Nusantara civilization (the historical culture of the Malay Archipelago) merit new application today. These principles have been foundational for their society, including the manner in which new religions are accepted and the relationships established among different religious communities. They have no desire to replace the pre-existing culture with something that supposedly arises purely from Islam.

The *Nusantara Manifesto* explains, "For thousands of years, Nusantara (the Malay Archipelago) has been a civilizational crossroads and home to a wide array of peoples, cultures and religious beliefs" (para 87). "This distinguishing characteristic of Nusantara society — i.e., the impulse to position wisdom, rather than dogma, as the central pillar of socio-cultural, religious and political life — enabled Nusantara civilization to embrace the essence of newly arrived religions; neutralize their potentially divisive effects; and transform religious pluralism into a source of social unity and strength, by cultivating humility, compassion and respect for others, rather than fear and hatred" (para 89).

This is a strong religious endorsement of a cultural tradition that did not arise from that religion. Religious endorsements of cultural traditions frequently include a claim that the culture is partly the result of that religion; nothing of that sort is mentioned here. Quite the opposite, these statements suggest that Nusantara culture positioned the pursuit of wisdom as the key to religion in a manner that contributed to their hermeneutic. Nusantara culture provides the filter through which Islam and other religions can be understood, evaluated, and applied. Anyone who takes such a stance is already committed to accepting religious pluralism as a social reality.

The *Nusantara Manifesto* includes a ringing endorsement of the Indonesian constitutional principle of Pancasila, which is seen as the political application of these principles of Nusantara civilization.[25] Pancasila includes officially recognizing several religions, which is a specific rejection of

---

[25] Pancasila has been a foundational principle of the Republic of Indonesia since its beginning in 1945. In includes five points. According to the Preamble to the Constitution, "the Republic of Indonesia which shall be built into a sovereign state based on [1] a belief in the One and Only God, [2] just and civilized humanity, [3] the unity of Indonesia, and [4] democratic life led by wisdom of thoughts in deliberation amongst representatives of the people, and [5] achieving social justice for all the people of Indonesia."

Muslim theocratic visions (whether described as a caliphate or a Muslim country) such as those found in the Pakistani legal code or in the ideology of ISIS.[26] The Humanitarian Muslims affirm "the Republic of Indonesia as a multi-religious and pluralistic nation state, based on the principles of Pancasila and *Bhinneka Tunggal Ika* (Unity amid Diversity)."[27]

Humanitarian Muslims are not shy about recommending Nusantara culture to the world. "As heirs to this noble civilization, which is under siege by an array of powerful forces — including the globalization of culture, geopolitical instability and the weaponization of religion for political purposes — it is time for Indonesians to awaken and reclaim our ancient heritage, not merely for ourselves but humanity at large. For the profound wisdom that lies at the heart of Nusantara civilization is desperately needed in a world where ethnic, political and religious differences so often lead to enmity and violence" (*Nusantara Manifesto* para 90). Indeed, in the Proclamation of Humanitarian Islam they even suggest that their experience can serve as a "pilot project" for a multi-religious nation-state (para 19).

4. Faith and reason

The *Declaration on Humanitarian Islam* quotes K. H. A. Mustofa Bisri, former Chairman of the Nahdlatul Ulama Supreme Council: "People often claim that reason and religion cannot be reconciled. That is completely untrue, and ridiculous. ... As I understand things, ulama [interpreters of Islam] should be intellectuals, and intellectuals should be spiritual. They must work shoulder-to-shoulder, seeking to revive, in our present day and age, the values exemplified by the Messenger of God (saw.)" (para 91).

Humanitarian Muslims do not define reason as the abstract thinking of the European Enlightenment proving the existence of the human self or the existence of God. They have two types of reason in view, one of which

---

[26] Indonesian law recognizes Islam, Protestantism, Catholicism, Buddhism, Hinduism, and Confucianism as officially accepted religions. Other world religions have a right to meet, but with a lower level of recognition, including Judaism, Jainism, Sikhism, Taoism, and Zoroastrianism. Tribal and indigenous religions are usually tolerated as cultural practices, though not recognized as religions. The situation is more difficult for groups that are often perceived to be heretical movements within a world religion, such as the Ahmadiyya and Bahai. See Adeney-Risakotta, 209-211. See also Paul Marshall, "The Ambiguities of Religious Freedom in Indonesia," *The Review of Faith and International Affairs,* Institute for Global Engagement (March, 2018), available here: https://www.tandfonline.com/doi/full/10.1080/15570274.2018.1433588.

[27] This quotation is from the concluding "Call to Action" of the *Nusantara Manifesto*.

is well-defined and the second of which may not yet be so well-defined. The first is an expansive definition of the academic work — really a vast research, publication, and educational program — which is needed to develop and communicate the new Muslim orthodoxy.

"*Ulama*, scholars, academic institutions and other intellectual communities should be encouraged to mobilize all available resources to address the most crucial issues associated with the crisis posed by the enormous disjunct that exists between the insights contained within classical Islamic orthodoxy and the context of modern civilization" (*Declaration on Humanitarian Islam* para 86). They go on to describe the needed work in such fields as the science of hadith interpretation, the development of new religious norms, and the assessment of contemporary civilization with its socio-political structures.

A second type of reason the Humanitarian Muslims emphasize in their ethics is the human capacity for civilization building by means of developing human potential; the unity of faith with this type of moral reason helps individuals and communities to flourish. The *Nusantara Manifesto* quotes President Wahid: "The greatness of traditional Islamic art and architecture — from the wonders of Fes and Grenada, to Istanbul, Isfahan, Samarkand and Agra — bears testimony to the long line of Sufi masters, guilds and individual artists who strove to ennoble matter, so as to transform our man-made environment into 'the veritable counterpart of nature, a mosaic of "Divine portents" revealing everywhere the handiwork of man as God's vice-regent.'" He continued, "The greatness of classical Islamic civilization — which incorporated a humane and cosmopolitan universalism — stemmed largely from the intellectual and spiritual maturity that grew from the amalgamation of Arab, Greek, Jewish, Christian and Persian influences."[28]

Wahid then added an astonishing comment that may be obscure to those not familiar with ancient Greek philosophy: "That is why I wept upon seeing Ibn Rushd's [also known as Averroes, 1126–1198] commentary on the *Nicomachean Ethics* [written by Aristotle, 384–322 BC] lovingly preserved and displayed, during a visit some years ago to Fes, Morocco. For if not for Aristotle and his great treatise, I might have become a Muslim fundamentalist myself" (para 148). Humanitarian Islam has not only consciously appropriated principles from Nusantara civilization; the movement has explicitly appropriated themes from the ethics of Aristotle as part of their understanding of what reason is.

---

[28]   President Wahid is citing Seyyed Hossein Nasr as quoted in Roloff Beny, *Persia: Bridge of Turquoise* (New York Graphic Society, 1975), np.

In Aristotle's ethics, humanity is portrayed as poised between two poles, humankind as it is and humankind as it may become if individuals and communities develop as they can and should. For humanity to reach its built-in goal (telos) and meaning, human potentialities must be actualized. An actualized potential becomes a virtue, such as courage, wisdom, or the pursuit of justice. What makes humans different from other entities is their capacity for reason and their social (sometimes called "political") nature; humans are rational and social creatures. For individuals and society to reach a condition of comprehensive flourishing (*eudaimonia* in Greek, sometimes poorly translated as "happiness"), people must learn to practice intellectual, social, and professional virtues.[29] The virtues are learned by practice in community, which is usually related to imitating role models. Many virtues can be described as the "golden mean" between two opposite vices; the proper use of reason enables individuals and communities to learn the way of virtue.[30]

By means of writing about Aristotle's ethics, Ibn Rushd helped introduce Aristotle to Muslim, Jewish, and Christian educators in the Mediterranean and European cultures. Aristotle offered an approach to ethics and life in society that was mostly acceptable to non-extremist versions of Judaism, Christianity, and Islam, as well as to people without defined religious beliefs.[31] It offered an ethically responsible perspective on the development of people, professions, and entire societies, designed to lead toward human flourishing. This approach to ethics was widely seen as an approach to moral reason that was compatible with faith among the theistic religions.

With such ideas in mind, President Wahid could weep tears of joy at seeing Ibn Rushd's book on Aristotle in a museum in Morocco. That book symbolized the unity of Islam with moral reason in such a manner that leads to civilization building and stands in stark conflict with all forms of religious extremism. This approach to the compatibility between faith and reason sets Humanitarian Islam apart from violent versions of Islam.

---

[29]   Christian theologians have frequently mentioned the similarity between the Greek notion of eudaimonia and the notion of shalom found in the Bible.

[30]   This brief summary of Aristotle's ethics is not derived from Ibn Rushd; it is from the primary sources interpreted in light of the books by Alasdair MacIntyre such as *After Virtue: A Study in Moral Theory* (University of Notre Dame Press; 2nd edition; 1984), *Whose Justice? Which Rationality?* (University of Notre Dame Press; 1988), and *A Short History of Ethics: A History of Moral Philosophy from the Homeric Age to the Twentieth Century* (University of Notre Dame Press; 1998).

[31]   Religious authorities often expressed concerns and cautions regarding Aristotelian ethics. For example, within Christianity one hears the concern that the people who pursue virtue might become proud before God and not recognize their sin.

5. Constructive political developments

Humanitarian Islam is distinguished from extremist versions of Islam by its acceptance of selected socio-political developments of the last two centuries. This principle flows from the view of practical reason already described, but the topic merits distinct attention.

The *Nusantara Manifesto* identified four key social and political developments which make our world different from that of previous centuries: "i) A complete transformation of the global political order; ii) fundamental changes in demography; iii) evolving societal norms; and iv) globalization, driven by scientific and technological developments that enable mass communications, travel and the emergence of a tightly integrated world economy" (para 108).

Until 200 years ago, and to a large extent even 100 years ago, much of the world's population lived in kingdoms or empires in which there was a supposed unity of a majority religion and the ruling power, though minority religions may have been tolerated. Within Europe, this was described as the "unity of throne and altar." Today most empires have passed away, replaced by nation-states that contain millions of immigrants of all religions and cultures, with those populations and states connected by intergovernmental organizations (such as the UN) and international businesses. The age of religiously defined empires, whether in Asia, Europe, Turkey, or the Middle East, is long gone.

Therefore, according to Humanitarian Islam, any desire to return to a Caliphate or to perpetuate a religiously defined nation, as displayed by Muslim extremism and also by some critics of Muslim extremism, is an impossible desire to return to a previous era which leads only to conflict, destruction, and death. Instead, Muslims should fully accept a different relationship between religion and society, including a critical endorsement of some societal transitions.

Recall that Humanitarian Islam accepts *selected* socio-political developments of modern global society. It does not endorse atheism, moral relativism, or hyper-individualism. Though religious pluralism is endorsed as morally legitimate, Humanitarian Islam does not call on governments or schools to ignore religious values, practices, and communities. Rather, it believes that people's lives should be shaped by the teachings of their religious communities. Their adherents fully accept the existence of multiple religious communities within one country, with the hope that those communities and their members can flourish together.

6. Tyranny and the will to power

The *Nusantara Manifesto* says, "In the absence of self-discipline, the innate human drive to seek pleasure and avoid pain — whether physical, emotional or psychological — fosters egotism, injustice and a relentless pursuit of power for the sake of personal gratification. From an Islamic perspective this is the root of tyranny, whether it manifests on an individual or collective scale" (para 50).

More succinctly, the desire for power creates tyranny, and tyranny is the most serious threat to society. The will to power is demonstrated in many religious movements. "Again and again, those who crave worldly power have manipulated religious sentiment in their struggle to maintain or acquire political, economic and military supremacy, and to dominate their rivals. This has led to untold suffering and loss of life, and precipitated the ruin of entire civilizations" (*Manifesto* para 68).

In personal communication, the representatives of Humanitarian Islam have promised to more fully explain their response to the desire for power. They intend to do so by articulating how people can instead pursue a path to achieving nobility of character. I am eager for them to make good on this promise.

7. An assessment

The Humanitarian Islam movement is addressing in a systematic manner some of the deep theological issues that have contributed to conflicts among religions and cultures. Their efforts constitute a major payment on the intellectual debt owed by Islam to the watching world. To do this, their thought leaders are utilizing a theological method which they see as intrinsic to classical Islam, even if that method has not been effectively used for some centuries. The movement is retrievalist in the sense of seeking to retrieve an ancient intellectual and religious heritage to develop orthodox Islam in a manner that correlates with a new era.[32]

---

[32]   In this sense, Humanitarian Islam can be compared with retrievalist movements in other religions and intellectual traditions in our time. In all the branches of Christianity in the twenty-first century one can see movements that seek to retrieve a spiritual heritage that was lost via a serious cultural or political misstep, whether that misstep was modernity, secularism, colonialism, theological liberalism, or faulty church/state relations. These religious retrievalist movements are interacting with intellectual retrievalist movements that seek to recover a lost philosophical heritage, such as that of Aristotle, Jan Amos Comenius, or "the classics" more generally.

This recovery of a classical theological method has, at its center, a clarification of the difference between eternal norms and historically contingent applications of those norms. The key word, "sharia," as they use the word, refers primarily to the higher sharia, the eternal norms, not to the contingent application of those norms. The continued use by Muslim extremists of contingent norms from a previous era, such as blasphemy laws and the corporal punishment of criminals, fails to use a proper Muslim theological method, leading to needless suffering and loss of life, conflict among Muslims and with non-Muslims, and the resulting Islamophobia. The desire for a new caliphate does not arise from an eternal norm, and the several attempts to form new caliphates have led to death and destruction. The proper application of eternal norms in our era includes the support of multi-religious states and freedom of religion.

The theological method and hermeneutic of Humanitarian Islam are organically tied to their positive assessment of Nusantara civilization, which, as they see it, posited the pursuit of wisdom and religious tolerance as keys to societal flourishing and true spirituality. Their theological method includes a strong endorsement of rationality for civilization building, for perceiving eternal moral norms, and for using this perception of moral norms to distinguish between positive and negative directions in the social and political developments of the last two centuries. This approach to rationality is understood in an openly Aristotelian manner arising from the endorsement and use of themes from Aristotle's ethics in medieval Sunni thought. Such an approach is radically different from those approaches to Islamic ethics that view the exegesis of the contents of Islam as the only way to know right and wrong, such as seen in the Open Letter of 2014. Given their simultaneous affirmation of classical human rights principles, the ethics of Humanitarian Islam are largely understandable, and potentially even acceptable, to many people who do not share their Muslim religious beliefs.

The theological synthesis of Humanitarian Islam is poised to promote societal and individual development in their communities, along with constructive relationships with other religions and cultures. The theological component of their movement could be strengthened by interaction with other retrievalist religious and intellectual movements, especially those seeking to reactivate Aristotelian or other elements of medieval thought and culture. I wish that in 2007 our seminary student and his religious brothers had fallen into the hands of Humanitarian Muslims, not those of extremists. The result would have been stimulating discussion leading to new intellectual and economic initiatives, not tragedy.

Evangelical Ethics in the West

There are parallels between certain themes in Christian ethics and key issues addressed by Humanitarian Islam. An elucidation will promote communication and future cooperation. We can begin with hermeneutics.

1. The relationship between law and grace

The apostle John summarized the key to the Christian hermeneutic poignantly under the headings of law and grace: "For the law was given through Moses; grace and truth came through Jesus Christ" (John 1:17). This can be regarded as central for how Evangelical Christians should interpret and apply the contents of their faith.

John wrote "law and grace"; others use the terms "law and gospel" as a synonym, assuming that grace is communicated and applied via the gospel and the related promises of God. There are nuances in the law/grace relationship. For example, John quoted Jesus in confrontation with religious leaders as saying, "Do not think I will accuse you before the Father. Your accuser is Moses, on whom your hopes are set. If you believed Moses, you would believe me, for he wrote about me" (John 5:45-46). According to John, Moses brings the accusations of the law, but Moses also promised someone who brought grace, namely Jesus.

The contrast between law and grace is not primarily about the time of origin of a text, such as Old Testament versus New Testament. "Law" is God's command about what to do or not to do; "grace" is his provision of undeserved acceptance and forgiveness in Jesus Christ as proclaimed in the gospel. Moses gave the law and promised a future grace given in Jesus; Jesus assumed the law given by Moses and fulfilled the promises given by Moses. The Bible (and all Christian teaching) is a combination of commands and promises; therefore, to echo Martin Luther (1483-1545), it is always urgent that Christians distinguish commands and promises, law and gospel.

The apostle Paul summarized the gospel: "God was reconciling the world to himself in Christ, not counting people's sins against them. And he has committed to us the message of reconciliation" (2 Corinthians 5:19). Regarding law, Paul wrote, "For the entire law is fulfilled in keeping this one command: 'Love your neighbor as yourself'" (Galatians 5:14). Later he added, "The commandments, 'You shall not commit adultery,' 'You shall not murder,' 'You shall not steal,' 'You shall not covet,' and whatever other command there may be, are summed up in this one command: 'Love your neighbor as yourself.' Love does no harm to a neighbor. Therefore, love is the fulfillment of the law" (Romans 13:9-10).

The complexity of how God communicates his law and accomplishes his grace provides the hermeneutic to interpret and apply Scripture and Christian teaching.[33] I invite Humanitarian Muslims to tell us if there is something comparable within their hermeneutic. At times in Christian history, God's moral law has been described as the expression of God's holiness, justice, or wrath, while the gospel has been described as an expression of God's grace and mercy; one could ask how this is similar to and different from the well-known saying of Mohammed that God's throne bears the inscription, "My mercy precedes My wrath."

In a similar manner, some Christian theologians have claimed that the relation between law and gospel is the same as the relation between letter and spirit, quoting 2 Corinthians 3:6, which states that God "has made us competent as ministers of a new covenant — not of the letter but of the Spirit; for the letter kills, but the Spirit gives life." It would be worthwhile to inquire if there are similarities to President Wahid's claim that Islamic mysticism "recognized the need to balance the letter with the spirit of the law."[34]

2. God's moral, ceremonial, and judicial laws

Christianity distinguishes among God's moral, ceremonial, and judicial (or civil) laws as they are found in the Old Testament part of the Bible. This is

---

[33]   Distinguishing law and grace (or law and gospel) has been a distinctive rediscovery of Evangelicalism since the Reformation. For example, Martin Luther claimed, "You will not find anything about this distinction between the law and the gospel in the books of the monks, the canonists, and the recent and ancient theologians. Augustine taught and expressed it to some extent. Jerome and others like him knew nothing at all about it. In other words, for many centuries there has been a remarkable silence about this in all the schools and churches. This situation has produced a very dangerous condition for consciences." Martin Luther, *Luther's Works*, ed. and trans. Jaroslav Pelikan, vol. 26: *Lectures on Galatians, 1535* (St. Louis: Concordia, 1963), 313. Luther also wrote, "Let every Christian learn diligently to distinguish between the law and the gospel" *Galatians*, 120. For more on the Evangelical rediscovery of the relationship between law and gospel, see Thomas K. Johnson, "Law and Gospel: The Hermeneutical and Homiletical Key to Reformation Theology and Ethics," *The Evangelical Review of Theology* (2019) 43:1, available here: https://www.academia.edu/38262994/Law_and_Gospel_How_the_Reformation_Applied_the_Bible.

[34]   In "God Needs No Defense," p. 32 in the Nusantara Manifesto.

both similar to and different from the distinction made by Humanitarian Islam between eternal norms and contingent norms.

In the classical words of the Westminster Confession (1646):

> "Beside this law, commonly called **moral**, God was pleased to give to the people of Israel, as a church under age, **ceremonial laws**, containing several typical ordinances, partly of worship, prefiguring Christ, his graces, actions, sufferings, and benefits; and partly, holding forth divers instructions of moral duties. All which ceremonial laws are now abrogated, under the new testament. To them also, as a body politic, he gave sundry **judicial laws**, which expired together with the State of that people."[35]

Some Christians question this threefold hermeneutic, claiming it is not found in the Bible. However, this distinction was not only characteristic of the Puritan Westminster documents. With slight variations, it was used during the Reformation by John Calvin (1509–1564) and in medieval Christian ethics by Thomas Aquinas (1225–1274), both of whom regarded it as a common distinction long known to Christians. Calvin and Aquinas assumed the similar distinctions used by Augustine (354–430) and Justin Martyr (circa 100–165); indeed, one of the earliest Christian books after the New Testament, the Epistle of Barnabas, sharply contrasts the moral and ceremonial laws (compare chapters 2 and 19). Jonathan Bayes argues that this hermeneutic was already used in some Old Testament passages, such as Proverbs 21:3: "To do righteousness and justice is more acceptable to the Lord than sacrifice." "Righteousness" refers to the demands of the moral law, whereas "justice" refers to the demands of the judicial law.[36]

---

[35] Westminster Confession of Faith, chapter 19, paragraphs 3 and 4, emphasis added, available here: https://www.pcaac.org/wp-content/uploads/2019/11/WCFScriptureProofs.pdf.

[36] Jonathan F. Bayes, "The Threefold Division of the Law," The Christian Institute, 2017, available here: https://www.christian.org.uk/wp-content/uploads/the-threefold-division-of-the-law.pdf.
Bayes illustrates how this same distinction is used within Jewish theology. His essay is excellent. The threefold hermeneutic found in the earliest sources of Christian ethics points to the way in which Christian ethics has long taken the relation between eternal norms and changing situations into account. Some recent books on Christian ethics have given more prominence to the relation between norm and situation, for example, Thomas Schirrmacher, *Leadership and Ethical Responsibility: The Three Aspects of Every Decision* (Bonn: World Evangelical Alliance, 2013), available here: https://iirf.eu/journal-books/global-issues-series/leadership-and-ethical-responsibility/.

This three-part hermeneutic enables Christians to regard commands such as "You shall not commit adultery" and "You shall not steal" as parts of God's eternal and unchanging moral law that all must obey. Ceremonial laws are clearly different, not to be directly applied in our time; for example, Leviticus 2:1–2: "When anyone brings a grain offering to the Lord, their offering is to be of the finest flour. They are to pour olive oil on it, put incense on it and take it to Aaron's sons the priests. The priest shall take a handful of the flour and oil, together with all the incense, and burn this as a memorial portion on the altar, a food offering, an aroma pleasing to the Lord." Judicial laws are also obviously different in content and directly intended only for ancient Israel. For example, Exodus 21:15–17 says, "Anyone who attacks their father or mother is to be put to death. Anyone who kidnaps someone is to be put to death, whether the victim has been sold or is still in the kidnapper's possession. Anyone who curses their father or mother is to be put to death." Cursing one's parents is always wrong; execution for this sin was only for a limited time and place.

In ancient Israel, a strict anti-blasphemy law was enforced, on occasion, by the death penalty. "Then the Lord said to Moses: 'Take the blasphemer outside the camp. All those who heard him are to lay their hands on his head, and the entire assembly is to stone him. Say to the Israelites: "Anyone who curses their God will be held responsible; anyone who blasphemes the name of the Lord is to be put to death. The entire assembly must stone them. Whether foreigner or native-born, when they blaspheme the Name they are to be put to death"'" (Leviticus 24:13–16).

At times, Christians have enforced anti-blasphemy laws, even to the point of execution. This was wrong. An improper hermeneutic was applied to the Bible. Almost all Christians have repented of this sin, even if not all are conscious of a better hermeneutic. There is much to learn from ancient ceremonial and judicial laws, but we do not teach Christians to obey them directly. The biblical ceremonial and judicial laws were contingent, in the sense of being directly applicable to a certain time in history. In contrast, not stealing, not committing adultery, not committing murder, not bearing false witness, not coveting are eternal principles to be taught today.

3. The natural moral law

The entire undertaking of Humanitarian Islam is an appeal to a universal ethical standard which their leaders expect both Muslims and non-Muslims to recognize, even if the source and nature of this standard are not always fully articulated. This appeal sets Humanitarian Islam apart from the types of Islam that can only exegete the contents of their religion to explicate claims of ethical truth. The standard to which such an ethical appeal is made has been called the "natural moral law" in Western Christian ethics.

When people argue, there is inevitably an appeal, perhaps implicit, to an ethical standard by which our actions may be evaluated. When the people share a religion, they may refer to a religious text and say, "The Bible says . . . " or "the Koran says . . . ." When people do not share a religion, the norm referenced may be less explicit; nevertheless, it is crucial. Normal people seldom say, "There are no standards, so do what you want." When we argue, we imply, "According to the standards which we both know, I am right and you are wrong;" never "Let's just fight like animals."[37] This unwritten standard is the natural moral law, sometimes abbreviated as the "natural law."

Within Christian theology, the natural moral law has been regarded as a part of creation, specifically as a part of the creation of the human mind in the image of the mind of God, with the result that humans can hardly avoid distinguishing between right and wrong and almost necessarily make similar assumptions about right and wrong (though perhaps denying this knowledge). Christian theology also regards the natural moral law as a prominent theme in God's ongoing "general revelation," God's speech to humanity which comes to all people through his creation in multiple ways. (God's general revelation is usually contrasted with God's "special revelation," God's speech to humanity in Christ and Holy Scripture.)

The natural moral law is so strongly assumed in the Bible that the assumption is rarely clarified. Such clarifications typically arise when believers do something which their pagan neighbors properly regard as wrong, showing that unbelievers sometimes respond to the moral law better than do believers. A painful example is when Pharaoh followed principles protecting marriage and truth-telling before confronting Abram for not following such principles (Genesis 12:10–20), which both assumed everyone should know.

In the twentieth century, some Protestant theologians mistakenly claimed that we cannot know God's natural law, some saying we should not even mention the topic. This mistake threatens the soul of

---

[37] This analysis of moral discourse is heavily dependent on C. S. Lewis, especially the first chapters of *Mere Christianity*. This book was published multiple times and is available in many languages. Here I am referencing pages 15-26 of the revised edition of 1952 (London and Glasgow: Collins). For an assessment of Lewis on this topic see Thomas K. Johnson, *Natural Law Ethics: An Evangelical Proposal*, Christian Philosophy Today vol. 6 (Bonn: VKW, 2005), 85-105, available here: https://www.academia.edu/36884239/Natural_Law_Ethics_An_Evangelical_Proposal.

civilization.[38] There is wisdom in the observations of Aristotle, the oft-cited hero of both Humanitarian Islam and of many generations of writers about Christian ethics:

> "It will now be well to make a complete classification of just and unjust actions. We may begin by observing that they have been defined relatively to two kinds of law . . . . By the two kinds of law I mean particular law and universal law. Particular law is that which each community lays down and applies to its own members: this is partly written and partly unwritten. Universal law is the law of Nature. For there really is, as everyone to some extent divines, a natural justice and injustice that is binding on all men, even on those who have no association or covenant with each other."[39]

Similar ideas were taught by many classical philosophers, including the Aristotelians, Platonists, and Stoics, in contending against moral relativism, represented in the ancient world by the skeptics, sophists, and Epicureans. All the participants in these ancient discussions knew that different communities have different particular laws and moral rules, which raised the question of whether there is a universal moral law that is binding on all people and communities. The relativists claimed there are no universal moral rules or legal principles, only ethical rules and civil laws that are established by particular communities. Aristotle argued that there are moral and legal principles which are binding on all people simply because they are human; these laws are binding because of the inherent authority of the laws (the nature of those laws), not because they are authorized by a community. To repeat Aristotle, there is "a natural justice and injustice that is binding on all men, even on those who have no association or covenant with each other."[40] This law is binding on all people because of its nature as a universal moral law, not because people belong to a particular community (an association or covenant in Aristotle's words).

---

[38]   See Thomas K. Johnson, "The Rejection of God's Natural Moral Law: Losing the Soul of Western Civilization," *Evangelical Review of Theology* 43:3 (2019), available here: https://www.academia.edu/39590583/The_Rejection_of_Gods_Natural_Moral_Law_Losing_the_Soul_of_Western_Civilization.

[39]   Aristotle, *Rhetoric*, Book 1, chapter 13. Trans. W. Rhys Roberts; edited by Lee Honeycutt. (Alpine Lakes Design, 2011), available here: https://web.archive.org/web/20150213075009/http:/rhetoric.eserver.org/aristotle/rhet1-13.html.

[40]   I share the opinion of Tarnas that much of classical philosophy was a complex attempt to overcome the nihilism which was perceived to arise from religious syncretism (especially polytheism) and moral relativism. See Richard Tarnas, *The Passion of the Western Mind: Understanding the Ideas That Have Shaped Our World View* (Ballantine Books, 1993).

In the New Testament, the apostle Paul sided with the natural law theorists against the moral relativists when the Christian message entered into Greco-Roman culture. He wrote, "When Gentiles, who do not have the law, do by nature things required by the law, they are a law for themselves, even though they do not have the law. They show that the requirements of the law are written on their hearts, their consciences also bearing witness, and their thoughts sometimes accusing them and at other times even defending them" (Romans 2:14–15). In this way, early Christianity adopted the moral philosophy of the Old Testament (of which the account of Abraham is one of many examples) and contextualized it in the Greek and Latin terminology of the Roman Empire.[41]

I have not yet seen a full explanation of the natural moral law from the thought leaders of Humanitarian Islam, despite their appeal to Aristotle; however, the comments of President Wahid about "underlying perennial values" and the descriptions of a Nusantara search for wisdom sound like references to the natural law, perhaps using different terminology. This may be an unfinished theme or a desirable clarification in their ambitious theological program. By comparison, I will offer more of a Christian perspective.

The church fathers of the first four centuries usually summarized the demands of the natural law with the "Golden Rule," do onto others as you would have them do to you. For example, Augustine wrote, "There is also a law in the reason of a human being who already uses free choice, a law naturally written in his heart, by which he is warned that he should not do anything to anyone else that he himself does not want to suffer; all are transgressors according to this law, even those who have not received the law given through Moses."[42]

Aristotle and Augustine taught the natural law for different purposes. Aristotle was pointing to the universal moral law as a basis for a civilized society, assuming the existence of many communities and cultures with different particular laws; Augustine was preaching that all people are

---

[41] Throughout the first sixteen centuries of Christian history, most philosophical writers assumed a unity of the natural moral law governing humans and the laws governing the rest of nature (creation). God was seen as the source of the unified moral order of the universe, including humans, animals, plants, and rocks. Only in recent centuries, probably as a part of secularism, have Christians sharply separated the natural moral order from the natural physical order. This topic merits reconsideration. It would be worthwhile to compare the older Christian notion of a unified natural moral/physical law with the Muslim doctrine of Sunnatullah.

[42] Augustine, Letter 157, paragraph 15; found in Augustine, Saint, Bishop of Hippo. Works. English. 1990 Part 2, Volume 3 of Letters 156-210, trans. Roland John Teske, ed. Boniface Ramsey and John E. Rotelle (New City Press, 1990), p. 25.

accountable to God, even if they do not yet acknowledge God. (Aristotle did not mention God or the gods in relation to the natural moral law.[43]) Nevertheless, as the discussion of Christian ethics unfolded, the two lines of teaching from Aristotle and Augustine were harmonized but distinguished.

In the centuries after Augustine, within Europe and the Mediterranean basin, Christianity grew from a persecuted minority to become the majority religion, sometimes even the official religion. This prompted a discussion within Christian ethics of the relation between the universal moral law and the civil or human laws of different countries. This echoes the problem addressed by Aristotle and classical philosophy but with important differences. The perceived threats to a humane religious and social life came not so much from moral relativism and cultural diversity as from the church and the state (or states) alternately seeking absolute power. These two different types of tyranny (religious and political) threatened human flourishing.

Thomas Aquinas was a crucial contributor among the Christian writers on ethics of this era (400 to 1650), most of whom had studied both the Bible and classical philosophy. Both Augustine and Aristotle were quoted by many; historians of Western ethics sometimes refer to this perspective as the "biblical/classical synthesis."[44] In his "Treatise on Law," Aquinas distinguished four types of law in a manner intended to overcome moral relativism, religious absolutism, and political absolutism. The four types are (1) eternal law, which is a universal idea which has always existed in the mind of God and is not distinct from God himself; (2) the natural law, which is the participation of the eternal law within human rationality, communicated to humanity by the creation of the human mind in the image of the divine mind, the light of reason which cannot be fully extinguished even by sin; (3) human law, which is framed by human lawgivers and given

---

[43]   Other Greek and Roman philosophers ridiculed polytheism and idol worship. Aristotle may have thought such religions did not merit mention in serious discourse.

[44]   The teachings of Aristotle began to play a larger role in Western civilization in the twelfth and thirteenth centuries, partly through the efforts of the Muslim philosopher Averroes Ibn Rushd. The terminology of a "biblical/classical synthesis" probably comes from Anders Nygren (1890-1978). Nygren thought such a synthesis was a mistake that would reduce the Christian perception of the full demands of agape love. My argument here is closer to that of H. Emil Brunner (1889-1966), Gustaf Wingren (1910-2000), and I. John Hesselink (1928-2018) who thought this synthesis was extremely important for understanding justice and public life. It could be tremendously beneficial to compare the biblical/classical synthesis regarding ethics and society with the synthesis of Muslim and Nusantara ethical and legal principles found in Humanitarian Islam.

to a particular community for the common good; and (4) the divine law, which is the special revelation of God in the Bible.[45]

Revolutionary themes were hidden in this medieval text. Though writing during "Christendom," which history teachers commonly portray as the period of European church–state unity, Aquinas did not claim that human law should be based on the "divine law," the Bible; moreover, his outline suggests that neither the state nor the church has ultimate authority to evaluate a human law. In a manner that is remarkably untheocratic and anti-autocratic, he argued that human law is to be derived from and evaluated primarily by the natural law. In technical language he claimed, "So too it is from the precepts of the natural law, as from general and indemonstrable principles, that the human reason needs to proceed to the more particular determination of certain matters. These particular determinations, devised by human reason, are called human laws."[46]

This means that laws coming from a king or government are to be evaluated by the principles of equity which God has built into human reason, but without giving ultimate authority to a church which is evaluating human law by means of interpreting and applying religious texts. Though he was a man of his times, this was a principled break with both theocracy and autocracy. He was a Christian who honored God as the source of law and reason, but not in a manner that had to exclude other religions, since it was not a religious institution that could evaluate human laws.

During the Reformation, the new Evangelicals, such as Martin Luther and John Calvin, did not carefully follow the precise terminology of Aquinas. They simply assumed the reality and importance of the natural law, as was common in the Bible. But their rediscovery of justification by faith alone (not by obeying the moral law) pushed them to clarify what functions God's moral law has. This theological need prompted their prominent contribution to this discussion: new clarity on the multiple legitimate functions of God's natural moral law. Luther taught that God's moral law has two special functions (in addition to guiding the lives of Christians). The first is the civic use of the moral law, which restrains sin enough to make life in society possible; the second is the theological use of the law, which reveals our sin to ourselves.[47]

---

[45]   See Johnson, *Natural Law Ethics*, 15-18.
[46]   Thomas Aquinas, "Treatise on Law," questions 90 -96 of the *Summa Theologica* I-II, trans. Fathers of the English Dominican Province (Benzinger, 1947), question 91, article 3. Republished online in *Classics of Political Philosophy*, available here: http://www.sophia-project.org/uploads/1/3/9/5/13955288/aquinas_law.pdf.
[47]   Luther, *Galatians*, 308, 309.

Calvin did not woodenly follow the terminology of Luther, but his teaching was remarkably similar. First, Calvin compared the moral law to a mirror that "warns, informs, convicts, and lastly condemns, every man of his own unrighteousness" so one sees the need for forgiveness.[48] He then added, "The second function of the law is this: at least by fear of punishment to restrain certain men who are untouched by any care for what is just and right," almost a repeat of Luther.[49]

In this manner the Reformation more clearly distinguished the dimensions of the biblical/classical synthesis which came through Aristotle from those which came through Augustine. The reasoning of Aristotle formed the basis for the civic use of the moral law; the reasoning of Augustine supported the spiritual use of God's moral law. On the question of how to order life in society, Calvin can be taken as speaking for the main Reformers: "There is nothing more common than for a man to be sufficiently instructed in a right standard of conduct by natural law."[50]

The purpose of this brief history is to invite further discussion with the scholars of Humanitarian Islam. Since antiquity in Western theology and philosophy, the natural moral law has been the conceptual key for how morally serious people have responded simultaneously to moral relativism, political absolutism, and religious authoritarianism. The terminology is not wooden, but the principles are important; the universal ethical standard merits high-level discussion across religions and cultures. It seems probable that Humanitarian Islam can articulate a theory and method of application of the natural moral law, perhaps using the terminology of the "higher Sharia" which sometimes appears in Muslim philosophy.

4. Ethical standards and human goods

Within Christian ethics there is a developing discussion of the relation between ethical standards and human goods which has significant parallels in the ethics of Humanitarian Islam. In Western civilization for 300 years it has been common to distinguish between those things which are good for people and those things seen as abstract duties, doing what is "right" regardless of consequences for people. In moral theory this is the contrast between utilitarian ethics (good results for someone, often described as

---

[48]   John Calvin, *Institutes of the Christian Religion*, ed. John T. McNeill, trans. Ford Lewis Battles (Philadelphia: Westminster, 1960), II, vii, 6.
[49]   Calvin, *Institutes*, II, vii, 10.
[50]   Calvin, *Institutes*, II, ii, 22.

pleasure) and deontological ethics (doing what is good in itself). But this sharp contrast has not seemed reasonable to many people in the theistic religions. The assumption of a unified divine origin of people (with their needs and normal goods) and of moral duties (which are mostly to other people) has often prompted Jews, Christians, and Muslims to see an internal link between ethical standards (abstract duties) and human goods (the results of good actions). For example, Moses is quoted as saying, "The Lord commanded us to obey all these decrees and to fear the Lord our God, so that we might always prosper and be kept alive," clearly connecting abstract duty to God with human well-being (Deuteronomy 6:24).

In his discussion of this question, Aquinas argued that there are definable human goods that correspond with God-given human inclinations, that the natural moral law commands us to protect these goods, and that good, enforceable human laws give more detail about how to protect these human goods. Commentators on Aquinas normally say these primary human goods are "life, procreation, social life, knowledge, and rational conduct."[51] To avoid a secularized misunderstanding of Aquinas, one should note that knowledge, in his definition, includes knowing the truth about God. His definition of social life includes the protection of private property.[52]

There is an astonishing similarity between Aquinas' definition of human goods and the definitions provided by the Sunni jurists Imam al-Ghazali (1058–1111) and Imam al-Shatibi (d. 1388), who are quoted in the Declaration on Humanitarian Islam of 2017. These Sunni jurists described five human goods — faith, life, progeny, reason and property — which should be protected by ethical norms, the *maqasid al-shari'ah*. This similarity reflects extensive interaction between Muslim and Christian scholars in the twelfth through fourteenth centuries, which occurred largely in France and southern Europe. They interacted with each other to the extent that

---

[51] For example, Mark Murphy, "The Natural Law Tradition in Ethics," *Stanford Encyclopedia of Philosophy* (2002, revised 2019), available here: https://plato.stanford.edu/entries/natural-law-ethics/. Since the time of Aquinas some Christians have interpreted the Ten Commandments as God-given rules to protect these vulnerable human goods.

[52] See "Treatise on Law," question 94, article 2. The "New Natural Law" theory offers a longer list of primary human goods, mostly by means of dividing Aquinas' categories into distinct parts. For example, John Finnis argues that the basic forms of human good, which he also calls "values," are life, knowledge, play, aesthetic experience, sociability (friendship), practical reasonableness, and religion. *Natural Rights and Natural Law* (Oxford: Clarendon Press, 1980), 59-99.

it is now difficult to know who influenced whom and who is quoting whom in many books or essays.[53]

A clarification of the human goods that has been articulately argued in the twenty-first century is that it is not only faith (or knowledge of God) which is a primary human good; freedom of religion should be described as a basic human good to be protected by moral and civil law.[54] Indeed, it may be wise to argue that freedom of religion should be at the top of the list of primary human goods, because of the way in which freedom of religion plays an important role in securing or promoting the other human goods.[55]

Primary human goods in medieval Christian philosophy:	Primary human goods in medieval Muslim philosophy:
1. Life	1. Faith
2. Procreation	2. Life
3. Social life (including property)	3. Progeny
4. Knowledge (including God)	4. Reason
5. Rational conduct	5. Property

The ethical standards by which the medieval Christian and Muslim scholars evaluated human law were not precisely written in a particular text, though all these writers spent large parts of their lives interpreting the religious texts of their respective traditions. One side (Muslim) references a transcendent or higher sharia, while the other side (Christian) references a natural moral law imprinted in the human mind made in the image of God which no one can truly claim not to know. The Muslim and Christian

---

53   For more background on al-Shatibi, see Ahmad al-Raysuni, *Imam al-Shatibi's Theory of the Higher Objectives and Intents of Islamic Law,* trans. from Arabic by Nancy Roberts; abridged by Alison Lake (International Institute of Islamic Thought, 2013).

54   Robert P. George, "Religious Liberty and the Human Good," *International Journal for Religious Freedom* 5:1 2012, 35-44, available here: https://www.iirf.eu/site/as sets/files/92052/ijrf_vol5-1.pdf.

55   Brian Grimm and Roger Finke have used social science research to argue convincingly that freedom of religion contributes to many other indicators of societal flourishing including economic growth, political freedom, freedom of the press, longevity of democracy, lower levels of armed conflict, and reduction of poverty. See, for example, *The Price of Freedom Denied Religious Persecution and Conflict in the Twenty-First Century,* Cambridge Studies in Social Theory, Religion and Politics (Cambridge University Press, 2011).

scholars came to astonishingly similar conclusions regarding the primary human goods which are to be protected by the application of religious and civil laws. The representatives of Humanitarian Islam have made these medieval claims prominent in their twenty-first-century proclamations in response to religious extremism; at the same time Western Christian philosophers have been reactivating the same topic because of a loss of an ethical standard by which one can evaluate civil law in fully secularized societies. After a pause of several hundred years, one must say, "Let the Muslim/Christian discussion continue!"[56]

---

[56] To avoid misunderstanding one must emphasize that within Christianity the discussion of fundamental human goods and the natural moral law have to do with standards in society, how we relate to each other in society, and how we organize society. This is distinct from salvation, how we relate to God, how Christians proclaim the gospel of Christ, and the life of the churches. Human goods and the natural moral law are related to what Martin Luther and John Calvin described as the "civil use of the law."

From Clash to Cooperation

In our situation in which many thoughtful observers have worried about a clash between Christian and Muslim civilizations leading to a third world war, seeing each act of aggression between Muslims and Christians as a step in this direction, there can be tremendous gain by simply telling the world that a major Christian body (Evangelicals) and a major Muslim body (Humanitarian Islam) can achieve peace with each other. This is not the peace of shared religious beliefs; it is the peace of compatible approaches to life in society based on similar approaches to public ethics. Though in past times Christians and Muslims sometimes defined their religions in territorial terms, promoting religiously defined countries or states, almost all Christians and many Muslims have changed or are now changing their views of the relation between religious communities and the state, without changing their central beliefs about how people relate to God. Outmoded views of the relation between religion and the state not only contributed to conflict and war; such views also caused many to use inappropriate methods to prevent conversions between religions. Now Christians and Muslims even have the possibility to talk about the ethics of religious persuasion and ethical ways of relating to people who convert out of our religious communities, themes hardly anyone could discuss a few centuries ago.

Though they may always understand God and relate to God in very different ways, Humanitarian Muslims and Evangelical Christians see life, family, rationality, a faith community, and an orderly social/economic life as fundamental human goods that lead to flourishing in this world. They know that these deep human goods are vulnerable, needing protection from various political, spiritual, and moral threats. They have similar convictions regarding universal moral standards that should influence religious and legal norms, all of which should protect human goods. This must be demonstrated intellectually, politically, in education, and in shared humanitarian efforts.

Though the conflict between Christianity and Islam has a long history, this does not mean it is inevitable or that it has to be eternal. One must recognize the degree to which prior conflicts have been closely tied to outmoded understandings of the relation between religious communities and states, precisely the issue that is now changing.

I wish to close by proposing specific practical steps, all of which can build on the shared principles explained in this paper. These are all proposals of what Evangelical Christians and Humanitarian Muslims can do together:

1. Joint academic events at which university scholars and school-teachers from both religious communities discuss how to teach questions regarding religions in society.
2. Joint publications leading to or flowing from such joint academic events.
3. Joint meetings of parliamentarians from both faith communities to cooperate in the development of civil law so as to protect the basic human goods that derive from our understanding of the universal moral law.
4. Working together to provide information about tools for business, government, and education that promote harmonious interaction among people from multiple cultures and religions.
5. Joint humanitarian aid programs.
6. Cooperation in addressing problems that government alone cannot readily solve, such as homelessness, human trafficking, drug addiction, natural disasters, and environmental problems.
7. Joint peace interventions in places where Christians and Muslims have been on the opposite sides of conflict.
8. Joint interventions in places where identifiable people groups have their entire future at risk.

Though not addressed at length in this paper, secularism, atheism, and moral relativism in the modern West have been partly fueled for at least 350 years by the perception that organized religions are a cause of war and oppression. The perception of religious extremism has fueled secularism. This perception has tended to marginalize religious ethics and religious communities, sometimes pushing religious believers to privatize their convictions. Religious identity has sometimes been weaponized against religious believers. The level of philosophical agreement discovered in this paper would warrant a concerted joint effort, which would require intellectual creativity by the thought leaders of Evangelical Christianity and Humanitarian Islam.

Appendix I: Beyond Freedom of Religion

As demonstrated above, when the fundamental principles of Humanitarian Islam are brought into interaction with corresponding principles of Christian ethics, one obtains an ethical and legal perspective that can respond to religious extremism and also respond to efforts to maintain religiously defined states which require a particular religious identity to be full stakeholders in the society. This means we have clear ways of explaining the moral wrongness of both religious extremism and religiously defined states, on the basis of which we can then engage in principled argument with people and groups who support such morally wrong relations between religions and society. Such public-square moral argumentation could be much more influential if conducted by official representatives of two major religious traditions that were once perceived to be in endless conflict with each other.

Such a joint methodology of explaining and arguing the moral wrongness of public actions can, I believe, also be applied to all the major causes of religious persecution. But religious persecution is seldom isolated from other problems in society. Religious persecution, as we usually observe it, is organically tied to many of the major human-caused threats to societal flourishing. Over a long period of time, a joint Muslim–Christian public voice presenting principled arguments against religious persecution could have an enormous global impact that extends to the many other problems that are commonly associated with religious persecution.

The Open Doors World Watch Monitor has identified eight "engines of religious persecution," the types of ideas, societal forces, and political movements that repeatedly lead to persecution and repression for Christians. Open Doors primarily represents Evangelical Christians, but its methods of assessment are not specifically Christian and can be used by anyone concerned for human rights. The engines of persecution they have identified should also be of grave concern to Humanitarian Muslims and to all mature religious communities; these engines of persecution are threats to human flourishing very broadly.

All the engines of persecution arise from individuals or groups of people making decisions that are morally wrong. Given the devastating results of religious persecution, a determined global effort to address these factors in any way possible is warranted. Here we glance at these engines, asking the reader to note that all involve people making wrong decisions.[57]

1. Islamic Extremism. "Islamic extremists range from extremist states that require sharia law, such as Iran or Saudi Arabia, to extremist movements that seek to impose Islam but through relatively peaceful means, such as the now-outlawed Muslim Brotherhood in Egypt. There are extremist groups that espouse violence to achieve their aims, such as Boko Haram in Northern Nigeria. And there are extremist households or individuals, which are the most effective in enforcing Islam's apostasy laws."

2. Religious Nationalism.[58] "This refers to an ideology that seeks to make a territory or a state exclusively the province of a particular religion. It sees its religion as utterly supreme over other religions and traditions, and sets a very clear national boundary on its militancy. In this respect it is distinct from Islamic extremism, which is always trans-national . . . . This engine refers more specifically, for example, to the Hindu nationalists in India, who use the ideology of Hindutva to justify their vision of a Hindu India. Or, to the nationalist Buddhists in Sri Lanka, who maintain all Sinhala people must be Buddhist lest they betray their heritage and country."

3. Tribal Antagonism. "This refers to the reality that when someone becomes a Christian they are often persecuted because they are seen to have turned their back on the traditions of their tribe. Sometimes the tribe may have its own religion, such as animistic tribes in parts of Africa. Or, sometimes the tribe may simply be a social or blood obligation that can act as strongly as the religious ties."

4. Ecclesiastical Arrogance. "This is where a church tries to impose its version of Christianity on everyone, especially other Christians, and

---

57   "What are 'Engines of Persecution'?" The quotations in this section are from this website: https://www.worldwatchmonitor.org/what-are-engines-of-persecution/.

58   The term "religious nationalism" is used with widely different definitions. The World Watch List is defining dysfunctional religious nationalism. Some religious movements describe themselves as nationalist because they claim their religion contributes to nation-building, with the expectation that other religions can also contribute to building their nation. This second type of religious nationalism is compatible with freedom of religion. It may be possible for religious movements that once promoted dysfunctional religious nationalism, claiming one had to belong to their religion to be a good citizen of their nation, to become healthy religious nationalists, positioning their religion and other religions to contribute to the development of their nation.

refuses to accept the validity of other traditions." A similar problem can be observed among the different versions of Islam.

5. Communist Oppression. "Communism is an ideology that seeks to bring about a classless paradise through the triumph of the worker and is utterly atheistic in its method. But it is also a system of control, where the state seeks to ensure the church is registered in order to control it. While the ideological drive of communism is fatally wounded today, the communist system of state control over the church remains especially in those post-communist states such as Russia and the so called 'Stans' of Central Asia. Today, there are four countries left that are still formally communist: China, Vietnam, Laos and Cuba, though it is hard to say how much of the ideology remains and how much is just the system of control staying in place."

6. Dictatorial Paranoia. "Dictatorial paranoia drives a political leader and the inner clique to dominate every aspect of society. The dictator is seized by fear that someone, somewhere, is plotting an overthrow. No one is allowed to organize outside state control."

7. Secular Intolerance. "Secularism can be understood two ways. There is the positive side: The state remains neutral, or secular, in the face of religion, refusing to favor one faith or denomination over another. Indeed, in this sense, state secularism is a legacy of the Reformation, where the Anabaptists, for example, regarded themselves as aggressive secularists. The negative side: Atheists insist all religion be expunged from public life and from crucial discussions about social issues such as sexuality, marriage, and human dignity. The state's historical neutrality no longer is deemed sufficient; instead, religious expression is seen as injurious to the public good. Aggressive secularists do not tolerate dissenting interpretations of how to conduct public life, and claim that all religious expression is by definition pathological. This engine is most powerful in the Western world."

8. Organized Corruption. "When societies contain elites like mafias that run extensive economic rackets, Christians can get targeted when their ethics threaten these rackets. An obvious example are the Latin American regions run by guerrilla armies who get their funds through drug trafficking. Pastors or priests who stand against the drug trade are threatened and killed. This engine is perhaps the most global of them all, as each society – especially where the state is weak or complicit – contains very deliberate and organized schemes to direct riches to an often violent elite."

These eight engines which power the persecution of Christians are also threats to the well-being of the Humanitarian Islam community. Indeed, they are many of the major threats to human well-being more generally, attacks on the primary human goods as described in both Muslim and Christian philosophy.

Evangelical Christians and Humanitarian Muslims should cooperate in a global strategy of moral reasoning to argue against such causes of religious persecution. This means convincing people that such actions are unethical, morally wrong. This should not be merely self-defensive. From the Christian side we will surely want to describe such an undertaking as part of our love for our neighbors and attempting to be light in the world. Humanitarian Muslims will surely want to add their own religious description and motivation of such cooperative efforts.

Appendix II: Christian Milestones on Religion and War

The conversion of the Roman Emperor Constantine to Christianity in 312 CE, along with the decriminalization of the Christian faith which followed in 313 CE, were important steps in the trajectory in which Christianity became the largest and sometimes official religion of Europe. This transition came immediately after a persecution (303-311 CE) during which Emperor Diocletian attempted to exterminate Christianity in the Roman Empire. However, only a century later, in 411 CE, Saint Augustine supported the efforts of the Roman Empire to use force to suppress (persecute) the Donatist heresy in the Christian churches in North Africa. In 100 years, one part of Christianity had gone from receiving to supporting religious persecution.[59] This established a damaging precedent with repeated echoes within Christian history.

Another milestone in this trajectory came on Christmas, 800 CE, when Pope Leo III crowned Charlemagne as "Emperor of the Romans." Charlemagne was called the "New Constantine," who ruled over the *Imperium Christianum*. Though all the participants in this transition had several motives, including an East/West balance of power in Europe between the Eastern Roman (Byzantine) Empire and a renewed Western Roman Empire, one of the motives was to have a Western European power block that could resist the Islamic nations on their southern border. The grandfather of Charlemagne, Charles Martel, was famous for defeating a Muslim army at Tours in 732 CE; the new Emperor had to walk in his footsteps. There was a division of power between Church and Empire, including continuous competition between Church and Empire in some spheres of life; nevertheless, having a specifically Christian Empire reduced freedom of religion for other religions (including Christian movements outside the main church) and helped set the stage for wars with religious motivations, such as the Crusades. The wars with religious dimensions included the devastating European wars of the sixteenth and seventeenth centuries.

The Peace of Westphalia of 1648 brought the Thirty Years' War (1618-1648) to an end. This war has been described as a "War of Religion" which contributed to the secularization of the West. Though this war was partly

---

[59] Let me assure the reader that I assess Donatism as a real perversion of Christian teaching, but the use of force to suppress a theological heresy was a disastrous precedent.

between Catholics and Protestants, there were both Protestants and Catholics on both sides in many major battles, and powerful Catholic France fought against the Catholic Habsburg Empire. It is more accurate to say the Thirty Years' War was religious in result rather than religious in cause. That result was a higher level of state control over the churches. A key principle of the Peace of Westphalia was cuius regio, eius religio, the one who reigns decides the religion for his domain. The reigning nobility was expected to allow limited freedom for other Christian churches, but this did not always happen, an unhappy milestone in church/state relations. Though Christian churches had influence on the reigning nobles, the cost was sometimes a high level of control of the churches by the state.

Despite this unfortunate mix of religion with various nations and empires, that is only one side of the story. For countless millions, Christianity was about knowing God and serving God, with little regard to the nation or empire. Every century saw new Christian movements, orders, and missions, many of which implicitly rejected the union of churches and states; others explicitly rejected the church/state union by teaching that faithful Christians may not work for a government, especially not in a military or police role. Some, such as Roger Williams (1603-1683) in Rhode Island, wrote principles of freedom of religion into law; others, such as Jan Amos Comenius (1592-1670), made bold proposals for renewing and reorganizing church, education, and the state.

The founding of the Evangelical Alliance in 1846 should be seen in this light, as an attempt to spiritually renew Western Protestantism in a way that connected churches in several countries with each other, thereby reducing the importance of the connection of those churches with their nations and their governments. From its first years, the EA (now called the World Evangelical Alliance) engaged governments on behalf of religious freedom for people who were not Protestants, signaling a complete break with notions of church/state relations inherited from the Peace of Westphalia.[60] Unfortunately, this other side of the story was not totally established in Christianity until 1918.

World War I (1914-1918) demonstrated that the relationship of Christianity to militarism was not solved. In the words of Philip Jenkins, "The First World War was a thoroughly religious event, in the sense that

---

[60]   See Gerhard Lindemann, *Die Geschichte der Evangelischen Allianz im Zeitalter des Liberalismus* (1846-1879); Theologie: Forschung und Wissenschaft Bd. 24 (English title translation: *The History of the Evangelical Alliance in the Age of Liberalism* (1846-1879). Theology: Research and Scholarship Vol. 24; Münster, Lit Verlag: 2011), 1064 pages.

overwhelmingly Christian nations fought each other in what many viewed as a holy war, a spiritual conflict."[61] The state authorities of all the primary nations on both sides in the war claimed that they were God's warriors fighting against the enemies of God, while similar views were common among the soldiers. In many battles, the soldiers on both sides could have used the same scriptures, prayers, and creeds in church, but they killed each other because government propaganda convinced many they had to protect their Christian countries. "All the main combatants deployed such [holy war ideological] language, particularly the monarchies with long traditions of state establishment — the Russians, Germans, British, Austro-Hungarians, and Ottoman Turks — but also those notionally secular republics: France, Italy, and the United States. More specifically, with the obvious exception of the Turks, it was a Christian war."[62]

For example, using language that has offended many for a century, the American Congregationalist spokesman Newell Dwight Hillis took his holy war teaching to its logical conclusion, that Satan's earthly servants must be annihilated; that meant that the entire German race should be exterminated. "In 1918, he urged the international community 'to consider the sterilization of the ten million German soldiers, and the segregation of their women, that when this generation of German goes, civilized cities, states and races may be rid of this awful cancer that must be cut clean out of the body of society.' America's Liberty Loan Committee distributed a million and a half extracts from Hillis's book."[63]

Lest one miss the point, as part of gaining popular support for US involvement in the First World War, a prominent Protestant minister advocated genocide, and this open Christian endorsement of genocide became part of the US government propaganda for participation in the war. The German soldiers he wanted to exterminate wore belt buckles with "Gott mit uns" (God with us) printed on them, while their understanding of God was shaped by German Protestantism. Only a century ago, this was a low point in church/state relations in the West. It sounded as if one group of Christian countries was destroying another group of Christian countries, all seeking to defend Christianity with the force of arms.[64]

---

[61] Philip Jenkins, *The Great and Holy War: How World War I Became a Religious Crusade* (HarperCollins: Kindle Edition, 2014), 4-5.

[62] Jenkins, p. 7.

[63] Jenkins, p. 11. Jenkins was quoting Newell Dwight Hillis, *The Blot on the Kaiser's Scutcheon* (New York: Fleming H. Revell, 1918), p. 59.

[64] Some American Protestant clergy took a radically different approach. For example, E. J. Tanis wrote *The Church, the Christian, and the War* (Grand Rapids: Louis Kregel, 1917), in which he claimed, "The Church, as an institution, and in her official

As is true of Muslims, most Christians are sickened to see their religion used to support killing. Soon after the first war, Christians in most of the branches of Christianity began to see religious support for excessive militarism as an indication that the spiritual life of their churches was in sharp decline. Attempts at spiritual renewal, often led by renewals of Christian theology, blossomed in most of the countries that participated in the war, with the primary exception of Russia, which was dominated by the Communist Revolution. This moral/spiritual transition prompted a reformulation of the assumption that there should be such an entity as a Christian empire or nation.

In the 1920s and 1930s, there were numerous calls for a renewed "Christian West," "Christian Europe," or "Christian America," with a view toward spiritual renewal that went beyond the realm of personal life and the church. However, these calls for a return to Christian civilization were different from such movements of a prior era; this difference is seen in the way in which these religious and cultural renewal movements were multinational and frequently crossed lines among churches that had little communication before 1920. By the 1920s, Christians who tried to kill each other as soldiers between 1914 and 1918 were praying together for the spiritual renewal of Western culture. Even when not explicitly rejected, older notions of a Christian Empire or of a close alliance of church and state were dropped as Christians from many states and churches engaged in spiritual fellowship with each other.

Seemingly in place of an expectation of the previous era, that a state would receive moral standards from its official or dominant religion, many Christian intellectuals from several countries and churches of the 1920s through 1940s began to discuss ethical standards that should apply to all people and institutions, regardless of religion. There were two main lines of discussion which often overlapped and intersected under the terminology of "universal human rights" and of a "natural moral law."[65] The notion

---

capacity, can take no part in the hostilities of war. She cannot preach sermons in which the wrongs of other nations are emphasized and the people wronged are aroused to retaliate. The German and English clergymen have been guilty of this sin, and it behooves the Church of Christ in America to guard against this error" p. 8. He continues, "The Christian sees in the present war, confined to the nations of Christendom, the righteous scourge of a just and holy God because of the present apostasy of the present generation" p. 10. Full disclosure: E. J. Tanis was the grandfather of my wife and was a spiritual hero in our circles.

[65]   These noteworthy thinkers included Jacques Maritain of France (1882-1973), Charles Malik of Lebanon (1906-1987), H. Emil Brunner of Switzerland (1889-1966), Dietrich Bonhoeffer of Germany, especially in his posthumous writings (1906-1945), and C. S. Lewis of the United Kingdom (1898-1963).

of a natural moral law was more difficult to popularize, but the notion of universal human rights provided theoretical language to articulate the moral revulsion felt by millions at the sight of two world wars and the Holocaust.[66] The adoption of the Universal Declaration of Human Rights by the United Nations in 1948, including its strong doctrine of religious freedom, signaled the end of the Constantinian era in Christian political ethics.

There was a long era, from the Donatist persecution of 411 CE till the end of the First World War in 1918, during which parts of Western Christianity included problematic themes in its approach to church/state relations. This included notions of a Christian Empire or nation, with various attempts at church-controlled states and state-controlled churches. These assumptions occasionally dominated political propaganda even in countries that had a legal separation of church and state, such as France and the US. Over a period of 30 years, from 1918 to 1948, Western Christianity finally dropped these problematic themes from its social teaching, replacing them with a doctrine of universal human rights, including the definition of freedom of religion in the UN Declaration of 1948 that protected the right of people to convert to other (non-Christian) religions. This is the same era that Indonesian Muslims, led by the Nahdlatul Ulama, began in 1926 to fully articulate their principles of religious toleration and pluralism. These developments in Christian and Muslim political ethics set the stage for Christianity to engage Islam in a manner that is totally different from the era of crusades and jihads.

---

[66] In the decades following 1948, United Nations human rights efforts and language became increasingly separated from the earlier fruitful interaction with the natural moral law. As a result, human rights were partly reduced from being a key component of a global moral compass to be an object of political manipulations. See Aaron Rhodes, *The Debasement of Human Rights: How Politics Sabotage the Ideal of Freedom* (Encounter Books, 2018).

Appendix III: Selections from the Sources of the Humanitarian Islam Movement

The Humanitarian Islam movement is publishing a series of public documents regarding its approach to the re-contextualization or reformation of Islam. Until this time (July 2020), two of these documents are longer and of a more foundational nature than are the other documents. These two documents are the *Declaration on Humanitarian Islam* of May 2017, and the *Nusantara Manifesto* of October 2018. The *Nusantara Manifesto* included, as an official appendix, the essay "God Needs No Defense" (*Tuhan Tak Perlu Dibela*) by H.E. Kyai Haji Abdurrahman Wahid, giving that text an official status within the movement. Serious students of Islam and of the foundations for human rights are encouraged to read these texts in their entirety. As an introduction, these excerpts are included as an appendix. These excerpts were selected by Thomas K. Johnson, not by a representative of the Humanitarian Islam movement. The paragraph numbers are taken from the original sources.

1. Gerakan Pemuda Ansor Declaration on Humanitarian Islam

Towards the Recontextualization of Islamic Teachings, for the Sake of World Peace and Harmony Between Civilizations

This Declaration was adopted at the International Gathering of Ulama ("Halaqah") held on 21 – 22 May 2017 at Pondok Pesantren Bahrul 'Ulum, Tambak Beras in Jombang, East Java.

The Context

1. In the theory of classical Islamic law (*usul fiqh*), religious norms (*akham*; singular, *hukm*) constitute a response to reality. The purpose of religious norms (*maqasid alshari'ah*) is to ensure the spiritual and material well-being of humanity.

2. The authoritative Sunni jurists, Imam al-Ghazali and Imam al-Shatibi, identified five primary components of *maqasid al-shari'ah*, viz., the preservation of faith, life, progeny, reason and property.

3. Religious norms may be universal and unchanging—e.g., the imperative that one strive to attain moral and spiritual perfection—or they may be "contingent," if they address a specific issue that arises within the ever-changing circumstances of time and place.

4. As reality changes, contingent—as opposed to universal—religious norms should also change to reflect the constantly shifting circumstances of life on earth. This was in fact the case during the early centuries of Islam, as various schools of Islamic law (*madzhab*) emerged and evolved. For the past five centuries, however, the practice of *ijtihad* (independent legal reasoning, employed to create new religious norms) has generally lapsed throughout the Sunni Muslim world.

5. When contemporary Muslims seek religious guidance, the most widely-accepted and authoritative reference source—indeed, the standard of Islamic orthodoxy—is the corpus of classical Islamic thought (*turats*)—and especially *fiqh* (jurisprudence)—that reached its peak of development in the Middle Ages and was then frozen in place, largely unchanged to the present day.

6. A wide discrepancy now exists between the structure of Islamic orthodoxy and the context of Muslims' actual (lived) reality, due to immense changes that have occurred since the teachings of orthodox Islam grew ossified towards the end of the medieval era.

7. This disjunct between key tenets of Islamic orthodoxy and the reality of contemporary civilization can, and often does, lead Muslims into physical, moral and spiritual danger, if they insist upon observing certain elements of *fiqh*, regardless of their present context. Among the complex issues that lie at the heart of this discrepancy are:

- Normative practices governing relations between Muslims and non-Muslims, including the rights, responsibilities and role of non-Muslims who live in Muslim-majority societies, and vice versa;
- Relations between the Muslim and non-Muslim world, including the proper aims and conduct of warfare;
- The existence of modern nation states and their validity—or lack thereof—as political systems that govern the lives of Muslims; and
- State constitutions and statutory laws/legal systems that emerged from modern political processes, and their relationship to *shari'ah*.

8. Social and political instability, civil war and terrorism all arise from the attempt, by ultraconservative Muslims, to implement certain elements of *fiqh* within a context that is no longer compatible with said classical norms.

9. Any attempt to establish a universal Islamic state—*al-imamah al-udzma* (the Great Imamate), also known as *al-khilafah* (the Caliphate)—will only lead to disaster for Muslims, as one aspirant battles with another for dominion of the entire Islamic world.

10. The history of Islam following the death of the Prophet's (saw.) son-in-law, Sayyidina Ali, demonstrates that any attempt to acquire and consolidate political/military power in the form of a Caliphate will inevitably be accompanied by the slaughter of one's opponents, and tragedy for the Muslim community as a whole, particularly at the outset of a new dynasty.

11. When this effort is fused with the orthodox injunction to engage in offensive war against non-Muslims—until they convert or submit to Islamic rule, so that the entire world may be united beneath the banner of Islam—this constitutes a summons to perpetual conflict, whose ever-widening appeal to Muslims is rooted in the very history and teachings of Islam itself.

12. Indeed, authoritative elements of *fiqh* describe such conflict as a religious obligation—which, at times, is incumbent upon the Muslim community in general, and others, upon every Muslim adult male, depending on the circumstances involved—for these religious norms emerged at a time when conflict between Islam and non-Muslim neighboring states was nearly universal.

13. If Muslims do not address the key tenets of Islamic orthodoxy that authorize and explicitly enjoin such violence, anyone—at any time—may harness the orthodox teachings of Islam to defy what they claim to be the illegitimate laws and authority of an infidel state and butcher their fellow citizens, regardless of whether they live in the Islamic world or the West. This is the bloody thread that links so many current events, from Egypt, Syria and Yemen to the streets of Mumbai, Jakarta, Berlin, Nice, Stockholm and Westminster.

14. Civil discord, acts of terrorism, rebellion and outright warfare—all pursued in the name of Islam—will continue to plague Muslims, and threaten humanity at large, until these issues are openly acknowledged and resolved.

15. Clearly, the world is in need of an alternative Islamic orthodoxy, which the vast majority of Muslims will embrace and follow.

16. The question that confronts humanity—Muslims and non-Muslims alike—is: how can we encourage, and ultimately ensure, that such an alternative not only arises, but becomes the dominant orthodoxy?

A Threat to All Humanity

25. The Islamic world is in the midst of a rapidly metastasizing crisis, with no apparent sign of remission. Among the most obvious manifestations of this crisis are the brutal conflicts now raging across a huge swath of territory inhabited by Muslims, from Africa and the Middle East to the borders of India; rampant social turbulence throughout the Islamic world; the unchecked spread of religious extremism and terror; and a rising tide of Islamophobia among non-Muslim populations, in direct response to these developments.

26. Most of the political and military actors engaged in these conflicts pursue their competing agendas without regard to the cost in human lives and misery. This has led to an immense humanitarian crisis, while heightening the appeal and dramatically accelerating the spread of a de facto Islamist revolutionary movement that threatens the stability and security of the entire world, by summoning Muslims to join a global insurrection against the current world order.

27. In other words, the crisis that engulfs the Islamic world is not limited to armed conflicts raging in various and sundry regions. Due to the transcendent value ascribed to religious belief by the vast majority of Muslims, the competition for power in the Islamic world necessarily includes a major sectarian/ideological (i.e., religious) component.

28. Various actors—including but not limited to Iran, Saudi Arabia, ISIS, al-Qaeda, Hezbollah, Qatar, the Muslim Brotherhood, the Taliban and Pakistan—cynically manipulate religious sentiment in their struggle to maintain or acquire political, economic and military power, and to destroy their enemies. They do so by drawing upon key elements of classical Islamic law (*fiqh*), to which they ascribe divine authority, in order to mobilize support for their worldly goals.

29. Mirroring this phenomenon, Western populists, Hindu nationalists and Buddhist monks in Sri Lanka and Myanmar often cite the identical elements of Islamic orthodoxy, and the behavior of Muslims, to justify their perception of Islam as a subversive political ideology, rather than as a religion deserving of constitutional protections and respect.

A Critical Juncture

31. Whether conscious or not, willing or not, Muslims face a choice between starkly different visions of the future. Will they strive to recreate the long-lost ideal of religious, political and territorial unity beneath the banner of a Caliphate—and thus seek to restore Islamic supremacy—as reflected in their communal memory and still firmly entrenched within the prevailing corpus, and worldview, of orthodox, authoritative Islam? Or will they strive to develop a new religious sensibility that reflects the actual circumstances of our modern civilization, and contributes to the emergence of a truly just and harmonious world order, founded upon respect for the equal dignity and rights of every human being?

48. The Wahhabi/ultraconservative view of Islam—which is embraced not only by Saudi Arabia and Qatar, but also by al-Qaeda and ISIS—is intricately wedded to those elements of classical Islamic law that foster sectarian hatred and violence.

49. Wahhabism is characterized by extreme animosity towards Shi'ites. It is also characterized by antipathy—at times violent—towards Christians, Jews, Hindus, Buddhists and Sunni Muslims who do not share the Wahhabis' rigid and authoritarian view of Islam.

50. In seeking to mobilize Sunni Muslims in opposition to Iran, Saudi Arabia has unleashed a demon upon the world, which threatens the temporal and spiritual well-being of Muslims. It does so by indoctrinating Muslims in religious hatred, and teaching them to ignore the primary message of Islam as a source of universal love and compassion (*rahmah*). The government of Pakistan has fallen prey to the same temptation, in its perennial competition with India.

53. It is essential to strip away the veil of illusion employed by state and non-state actors, whenever and wherever they seek to instrumentalize Islam to pursue their political, economic and military interests.

54. Those who overtly and/or covertly employ problematic tenets of *fiqh* to achieve their worldly objectives must be held accountable and, whenever possible, required to alter their behavior.

55. Iran, Saudi Arabia and Qatar do not tolerate foreign interference in their domestic affairs, especially in regard to religion and politics. No nation in the world should tolerate, nor be subjected to, interference in its domestic affairs by the governments of Saudi Arabia, Qatar or Iran.

56. Saudi opposition to Iran, ISIS and al-Qaeda does not and should not absolve it from responsibility for promoting the very ideology that underlies and animates Sunni extremism and terror.

57. The temporal and spiritual welfare of Muslims, and humanity at large, requires that Saudi Arabia abandon the "global Wahhabization/radicalization" strategy it has employed, to date, in seeking to contain Iran. It is a fundamental principle of Sunni Islam not to employ evil means to address problems caused by evil.

2. The Nusantara Manifesto

Launching the Recontextualization (i.e., Reform) of Obsolete and Problematic Tenets Within Islamic Orthodoxy

> *A call to people of goodwill of every faith and nation*
> *to join in building a global consensus*
> *to prevent the political weaponization of Islam,*
> *whether by Muslims or non-Muslims,*
> *and to curtail the spread of communal hatred*
> *by fostering the emergence of a truly just and harmonious world order,*
> *founded upon respect for the equal rights and dignity*
> *of every human being.*

This Manifesto was officially adopted and promulgated by Gerakan Pemuda Ansor and Bayt ar-Rahmah at the Second Global Unity Forum, held in Yogyakarta, Indonesia, on October 25 and 26, 2018. It builds on the claims presented in the *Declaration of Humanitarian Islam*, especially points 1 to 8 above. The Manifesto is forty pages in length; only some high points are reproduced here.

9. In the words of Kyai Haji Yahya Cholil Staquf, General Secretary of the Nahdlatul Ulama Supreme Council: "The Nusantara Manifesto represents a concrete step whereby Gerakan Pemuda Ansor and Bayt ar-Rahmah are officially, and institutionally, initiating a process to bring problematic elements of Islamic orthodoxy into alignment with the 'civilizational realities' of the 21st century."

14. A rising tide of Islamism in its myriad forms—which run the gamut from *preman berjubah* (thugs draped in Arab garb) to social media activists, proselytism movements, educational networks, political parties and even terrorist groups affiliated with al-Qaeda and the Islamic State—has been among the most noteworthy phenomena to emerge in Indonesia over the past 20 years.

15. Individually and collectively, these developments threaten the unity of Indonesia and its people, often in ways more subtle and profound than the bloody conflicts waged in the name of Islam in regions as diverse as Ambon, Poso and Aceh.

16. And yet, this threat is far from new. Both before and after Indonesia achieved independence, its founding fathers had to grapple with the tension that exists between Islamic orthodoxy and the ideals of the modern nation state. In June 1945, the members of the Preparatory Committee for

Independence (PPKI) reached a temporary consensus with the Jakarta Charter, which subsequently formed the basis for the preamble to the Constitution of Indonesia. It originally included an obligation for Muslims to abide by Islamic law (shari'ah).

17. In the course of further negotiation, secular Muslim nationalists, including Soekarno and Muhammad Hatta, persuaded their fellow committee members to delete seven words— "with Muslims required to observe Islamic law"—from the first principle of Pancasila, the foundational political philosophy of the newly-independent Indonesia. Hatta argued convincingly that Hindu- and Christian-dominated regions of the East Indies would refuse to join the Republic of Indonesia if its Constitution were to contain the seeds of an Islamic state.

18. Yet, although the committee members unanimously adopted the 1945 Constitution (UUD-45), the tension reflected in their debate over the Jakarta Charter has never been resolved and continues to roil Indonesian society to the present day.

19. The election of a Constitutional Assembly, in 1955, witnessed the reemergence of this fierce debate regarding what form of government Indonesia should adopt: Islamic theocracy or a secular nation state. After years of political maneuvering and conflict, in July of 1959 President Soekarno wielded an iron fist to end the debate, by dissolving the Constitutional Assembly and re-imposing the 1945 Constitution via presidential decree.

20. In addition to paralyzing legislative conflict, the 1950s were also a time of armed rebellions waged in the name of Islam. From 1949 – 1962 the Darul Islam/ Tentara Islam Indonesia (Islamic State/Indonesian Islamic Army) movement flourished in West Java, South Sulawesi, South Kalimantan and Aceh. DI/TII recognized only shari'ah as a valid source of law, while terrorizing and beheading its opponents. In Sumatra and Sulawesi, the Revolutionary Government of the Republic of Indonesia (PRRI) raised the banner of Islam, due to the fact that the Islamist party Masyumi—stung by its political defeat at the hands of Soekarno, Kyai Wahab Hasbullah (Chairman of the Nahdlatul Ulama) and other Indonesian nationalists—was deeply involved in the CIA-backed PRRI/Permesta rebellion (1958 – 1961).

21. These historical experiences demonstrate that Islamism—especially as a political movement based on religious identity—is indeed a latent, enduring threat to the existence of the Unitary State of the Republic of Indonesia (NKRI) as a multi-religious and pluralistic (Pancasila) nation state.

22. Under the Soeharto regime, this threat was repressed continuously and with considerable difficulty, but never completely neutralized. The rising tide of Islamism in post-Soeharto Indonesia may thus be said to

constitute a "rebound" of the perennial Islamist aspiration and its accompanying pressure to transform Indonesia from a Pancasila nation state to an Islamic state.

23. Social groupings based on religious identity are a natural phenomenon. The problem with certain tenets of Islamic orthodoxy lies in the fact that these invariably incarnate as a form of political identity, with a marked tendency to embrace absolutism and a hidden or explicit agenda of dominating the existing political order, whatever that may happen to be. Whether this struggle to acquire political supremacy is waged blatantly or covertly is simply a matter of strategy and tactics.

24. Detailed analysis—including careful study of the historical dimensions of this phenomenon—may be necessary to gain comprehensive understanding of this issue. Yet one thing cannot be denied: the aspiration for Islam to attain political domination is indeed an intrinsic part of orthodox Islamic teachings, if we employ the term "Islamic orthodoxy" to describe "an array of theological doctrines accepted by the majority of Muslims as the most authoritative religious reference standard."

25. And how could this not be the case? Islamic orthodoxy includes a remarkably extensive discourse about public law, both civil and criminal, which is generally described as "God's law" (*sharī'ah*)—or at least as "the interpretation of God's law" (*fiqh*)—which must be implemented in daily life. Obviously, this cannot be achieved without political domination by those who wish to implement *sharī'ah* (in reality, *fiqh*), which describes the Islamist agenda precisely.

26. Soeharto viewed Islamist political pressure as a threat to his own power. Hence, he adopted a strategy of political and military repression, combined with symbolic concessions carefully negotiated in order to pacify the Islamist groups. The products of these negotiations are clearly visible in post-Soeharto Indonesia: the embedding of religious education within the school curriculum; the establishment of the Indonesian Ulama Council (MUI); the creation of an Islamic judicial system that exercises jurisdiction over marriage, divorce, remarriage and inheritance solely for Muslims; "political donations" offered to compliant Islamic institutions and organizations; the establishment of "*sharī'ah*-compliant" banks; and the creation and government support of the Association of Indonesian Muslim Intellectuals (ICMI), to name a few.

27. And yet, like Muhammad Ali of Egypt, Ataturk and the Pahlavis of Iran, the Soeharto regime failed to address the problematic tenets within Islamic orthodoxy that underlie and animate the perennial Islamist threat, which can only be done through a process of recontextualizing, or reforming, Islamic orthodoxy itself.

28. Throughout its history, the Nahdlatul Ulama (NU) has been fortunate to possess leaders who strongly favored the Indonesian nation state over theocracy and genuinely yearned for the well-being and political success of NKRI. Among the most prominent of these NU leaders were Abdul Wahab Hasbullah and Abdurrahman "Gus Dur" Wahid. Both employed their religious authority as chairmen of the world's largest Islamic organization to mobilize their followers and maneuver strategically in ways that proved crucial to the survival of NKRI, Pancasila and the 1945 Constitution in truly desperate times.

29. During the 1950s and '60s, Kyai Wahab blocked Masyumi from restoring the Jakarta Charter and transforming Indonesia into an Islamic state; supported Soekarno and the Indonesian military in repressing the Darul Islam and PRRI/Permesta rebellions; and allied with Soeharto to prevent a communist seizure of power, such as that which had already occurred to such devastating effect in Russia, Eastern Europe, Central Asia, China, North Korea and Tibet.

30. During the 1980s and 1990s, Gus Dur mobilized the NU to help ensure Indonesia's successful transition from authoritarianism to democracy, and thus saved his nation from the fate that engulfed Syria, Yemen and Libya, and destroyed the fragile shoots of democracy in Egypt and Russia.

31. Kyai Wahab and Gus Dur encouraged other NU elites to develop a religious discourse that offered a concrete alternative to the obsolete, problematic tenets of Islamic orthodoxy. This alternative Islamic discourse has strengthened the legitimacy of NKRI, Pancasila, the 1945 Constitution and *Bhinneka Tunggal Ika*—Indonesia's national motto of "Unity Amid Diversity"—and mobilized the great mass of NU followers at the grassroots level to support this alternative discourse. But the "task" Kyai Wahab, Gus Dur and their followers have undertaken is far from complete. As Gus Dur himself remarked, "[We] must maintain a continuous dialogue between Islam and the Constitution."

36. So long as obsolete, medieval tenets within Islamic orthodoxy remain the dominant source of religious authority throughout the Muslim world, Indonesian Islamists will continue to draw power and sustenance from developments in the world at large. This is especially true so long as key state actors—including Iran, Turkey, Saudi Arabia, Qatar and Pakistan—continue to weaponize problematic tenets of Islamic orthodoxy in pursuit of their respective geopolitical agendas.

37. These considerations have led key figures within the NU—including Gus Dur in the months and years prior to his death, and former NU Chairman Kyai Haji A. MustofaBisri—to conclude that it would be impossible to

permanently resolve the tension that is inherent between Islamic orthodoxy and NKRI/UUD-45, so long as we confine our efforts to the domestic,
or purely Indonesian, context of the perennial Islamist threat.

38. Preserving Indonesia's unique civilizational heritage—which gave
birth to NKRI as a multi-religious and pluralistic nation state—requires the
successful implementation of a global strategy to develop a new Islamic
orthodoxy that reflects the actual circumstances of the modern world in
which Muslims must live and practice their faith.

40. The recontextualization and reform of Islamic orthodoxy is thus
crucial to the welfare of Muslims and non-Muslims alike, for it constitutes
the one indispensable prerequisite of any rational and humane solution to
the multi-dimensional crisis that has plagued the Muslim world for over a
century and not only shows no sign of abating—despite an ever-growing
toll of human lives and misery—but rather, increasingly threatens to spill
over and engulf humanity as a whole.

Religion, Tribalism and Secular Ideology

65. Throughout history, human beings have displayed astonishingly diverse behavior—both noble and, conversely, cruel and ignoble—while acting in the name of religion.

66. Every major religious tradition enjoins its followers to observe a
common set of humane and ethical standards, quite similar to those described above in regard to Islam.

67. Yet for thousands of years humanity has been plagued by discord,
animosity and violence perpetrated in the name of religion, which in turn
often constitutes a de facto ethnic or "tribal" identity.

68. Again and again, those who crave worldly power have manipulated
religious sentiment in their struggle to maintain or acquire political, economic and military supremacy, and to dominate their rivals. This has led
to untold suffering and loss of life, and precipitated the ruin of entire civilizations.

69. This raises a fundamental question regarding the nature and practice of religion, whose ramifications for modern civilization we may seek
to ignore but cannot escape.

70. As Dr. Rüdiger Lohlker observed in his essay, "Theology Matters:
the case of jihadi Islam": "Flatly denying the importance of religion causes
many in the West to overlook a crucial element of jihadi thought and action. This is particularly evident with regard to the mantra so often repeated in the wake of each new terrorist attack, viz.: 'Islam is the religion
of peace.' The claim that religion motivates only positive behavior among

human beings, and the implicit denial that religion may ever legitimize negative behavior, cannot withstand intellectual scrutiny. History provides countless examples of both positive and negative behavior legitimized by religion . . . .

> "The only way to deconstruct this violent form of religion is to develop alternative forms of religion capable of resisting the theology of violence, which is characterized by apologetics that simultaneously demand and legitimize authoritarianism, socio-cultural and religious homogeneity, and the strict demarcation of boundaries, etc. [i.e., tyranny]."

78. Nevertheless, the ease with which Islamists have been able to exploit problematic elements of Islamic orthodoxy to clothe their political agenda in religious authenticity has had the far-reaching and catastrophic result of strengthening dogmatic forces worldwide. The full ramifications of this process are still unfolding and threaten to produce an enduring radicalization of politics on a global level. This is a particularly alarming development, as it comes at a time when the diverse peoples, cultures and civilizations of the world are increasingly interconnected, interdependent and interfused.

79. In the Islamic world and those regions with localized Muslim majorities, Islamist groups have used the clarion call of establishing an Islamic state to launch civil wars, insurgencies and campaigns of terrorism that have left cities in ruin, countless dead and millions displaced over a vast arc of territory stretching from the Western Sahel to the Southern Philippines. Many of these conflicts have lasted for decades and, in spite of their terrible toll, show no sign of abating in the decades to come.

80. The widespread perception of Muslims and Islam as a threat to non-Muslim societies is a direct and intentional result of Islamist groups' actions, and their astute use of propaganda, which transmits powerfully symbolic images of the dystopian reality they seek to create. Horrors of the past such as slavery, crucifixion and the public execution of alleged homosexuals, adulterers, infidels, apostates and magicians are resurrected, reinstituted as valid components of an Islamic social order and broadcast to a disgusted global audience.

Transcendent and Historically-Contingent Elements
of Religious Orthodoxy

(Thawābit and *Mutaghayyirāt)*

99. The majority of political conflicts within the Islamic world—and between Muslims and non-Muslims globally—stem from the Muslim world's failure to adapt, peacefully and harmoniously, to the realities of our current world civilization.

100. One factor that contributes to this failure—indeed, perhaps the primary factor—is a dominant mindset among Muslims, which tends to view the classical orthodoxy of Islam as an unchangeable set of religious rules and guidance.

101. Those who consider Islamic teachings to be immutable are, by definition, incapable of responding to the ever-changing circumstances of life in an appropriate and effective manner. They fail to apprehend the complex nature of Islamic orthodoxy, which evolved over a number of centuries in response to divine revelation and historical—i.e., sociocultural, political and military—circumstances encountered by Muslim communities in the broader Middle East and North Africa.

102. As the majority of 'ulamā' (Muslim scholars) have traditionally recognized, Islamic orthodoxy consists of both transcendent (i.e., immutable) elements (*thawābit*) and contingent responses to historical reality (*mutaghayyirāt*), which may be adapted to address and reflect the ever-changing circumstances of life.

103. In order to appreciate this analytical distinction, it is necessary to differentiate between the spiritual (i.e., essential) values of Islam and its contingent expressions, including numerous tenets of Islamic orthodoxy that emerged within the context of Islamic civilization in the Middle East.

104. The transcendent (immutable) elements of Islam include a perennial set of messages embedded within scripture as guidelines (also known as *sharī'ah*) that apply to all Muslims throughout space and time. These eternal values may be described as the religion of Islam, if we wish the term religion (*al-dīn*) to refer to that which is noble and enduring.

105. Temporal elements within Islamic orthodoxy, on the other hand, constitute historically-determined responses to specific circumstances on the part of Muslims. These responses may be described as the historical (or civilizational) manifestation of Islam, which occurred within specific territories at specific points in time, primarily within the Arab, Persian and Turkish cultural basins, often in response to armed conflict with neighboring states and the administration of conquered territories and peoples.

106. Islamic orthodoxy contains internal mechanisms, including the science of *uṣūl al-fiqh*—the methodology of independent legal reasoning employed to create Islamic law, or *fiqh* (often conflated with *sharīʿah*)—that allow Muslim scholars to adjust the temporal elements of religious orthodoxy in response to the ever-changing circumstances of life. These internal mechanisms entail a process of independent legal reasoning known as *ijtihād*, which fell into disuse among Sunni Muslim scholars approximately five centuries ago.

107. If Muslims are to live at peace with themselves and the modern world, it is essential that we recognize and acknowledge that the context of our current global civilization is profoundly different from that in which the religion of Islam was revealed to the Prophet Muhammad, may the peace and blessings of God be upon him, and the circumstances in which the temporal elements of Islamic orthodoxy emerged and gradually became ossified towards the end of the medieval era.

121. Certain tenets of Islamic orthodoxy emerged within the context of prolonged military conflict between Muslim and non-Muslim states. For example, one of the fundamental norms of Islamic orthodoxy is the assumption that a state of enmity exists between Muslims and non-Muslims.

122. It is not difficult to understand the origin and persistence of this particular tenet. From the persecution of early Muslims in the city of Mecca until the modern era, this norm may have served to ensure the survival and prosperity of Muslims, whose political entities—and, consequently, their enjoyment of full legal status within an Islamic state—were threatened by neighboring non-Muslim states. In this pre-modern context, it was necessary for the survival of Muslim communities, and of an Islamic state, that Muslims be constantly alert to the military threat posed by non-Muslim neighboring states and, by implication, non-Muslims who were allowed to dwell within their own borders.

Bibliography on Humanitarian Islam

Foundational documents in chronological order:

ISOMIL Nahdlatul Ulama Declaration, 2016; media report: https://baytarrahmah.org/2016_05_10_isomil-nahdlatul-ulama-declaration/; full text of the declaration: https://www.baytarrahmah.org/media/2016/Nahdlatul-Ulama-Declaration_05-10-16.pdf.

The Global Unity Forum and Ansor Declaration, 2016; https://baytarrahmah.org/2016_05_12_global-unity-forum-and-ansor-declaration/.

The GP Ansor *Declaration on Humanitarian Islam*, 2017; https://baytarrahmah.org/2017_05_22_ansor-declaration-on-humanitarian-islam/.

The Nusantara Statement, 2018; https://www.baytarrahmah.org/media/2018/Nusantara-Statement.pdf.

The Nusantara Manifesto, 2018; https://baytarrahmah.org/2018_10_25_nusantara-manifesto/.

The Findings of the 2019 National Conference of Nahdlatul Ulama Religious Scholars: Nahdlatul Ulama Abolishes the Legal Category of "Infidel" within Islamic Law; https://baytarrahmah.org/2019_10_16_world-first-nahdlatul-ulama-abolishes-the-legal-category-of-infidel-within-islamic-law/. The foundational text described in this article is entitled "Decree: Bahtsul Masa'il Ad-Diniyyah Al-Maudluiyyah;" https://www.baytarrahmah.org/media/2019/2019-Munas_Findings-of-Bahtsul-Masa%E2%80%99il-Maudluiyyah.pdf.

Resolution on Universal Human Fraternity and Global Civilization, 2019; https://www.baytarrahmah.org/media/2019/IDC-CDI_Resolution-on-Human-Fraternity-and-Global-Civilization.pdf.

Resolution on ethics and values that should guide the exercise of power, 2019; https://www.baytarrahmah.org/media/2019/CDI_Resolution-on-ethics-and-values-that-should-guide-the-exercise-of-power.pdf.

Resolution on promoting a rules-based international order founded upon universal ethics and humanitarian values, 2020; https://www.baytarrahmah.org/media/2020/CDI_Resolution-on-promoting-a-rules-based-international-order-founded-upon-universal-ethics-and-humanitarian-values.pdf.

Additional primary sources in chronological order:

Abdurrahman Wahid, "Right Islam vs. Wrong Islam: Muslims and non-Muslims must unite to defeat the Wahhabi ideology," *The Wall Street Journal*, 30 December 2005; https://www.wsj.com/articles/SB113590649048834335.

Abdurrahman Wahid, editor, *The Illusion of an Islamic State: How an Alliance of Moderates Waged a Successful Campaign Against Radicalization and Terrorism in the World's Largest Muslim-Majority Country.* Prologue & Preface: Prof. Dr. Ahmad Syafii

Maarif and C. Holland Taylor; Epilogue: Kyai Haji A. Mustofa Bisri; Principal Au-thors/Editorial Team: Kyai Haji Hodri Ariev, Prof. Dr. Ratno Lukito, and C. Hol-land Taylor. English translation by C. Holland Taylor. (Jakarta, Winston-Salem, Cairo, and Leiden: LibForAll Foundation, 2011), 597 pp. Portions of this book are available online: https://www.baytarrahmah.org/media/2011/The-Illusion-of-an-Islamic-State_Sample-Chapters.pdf.

Abdurrahman Wahid, "God Needs No Defense," foreword to Paul Marshall and Nina Shea, *Silenced: How Apostasy and Blasphemy Codes are Choking Freedom Worldwide* (Oxford University Press, 2011), xvii to xxii; https://www.baytarrahmah.org/media/2011/Silenced_God-Needs-No-Defense.pdf.

A. Mustofa Bisri and C. Holland Taylor, "Indonesia's 'big idea': Resolving the bitter global debate on Islam," *Strategic Review* 2:3, July – September 2012, pp. 34-43; http://www.iiqs.org/media/Strategic-Review_Indonesia-s_Big_Idea.pdf.

Yahya Cholil Staquf, "How Islam learned to adapt in 'Nusantara,'" *Strategic Review* 5:2, April – June 2015, pp. 18-28; https://www.baytarrahmah.org/media/2015/Stra tegic-Review_How-Islam-learned-to-adapt-in-Nusantara_Apr-Jun-2015.pdf.

A. Mustofa Bisri, "The Universal Values of Indonesian Islamic Civilization," *Strategic Review* 7:1, January – March 2017, pp. 36-45; https://www.libforall.org/lfa/me dia/2017/Strategic-Review_Universal-values-of-Indonesian-Islamic-civilization _Jan-Mar-2017.pdf.

Yahya Cholil Staquf, "Terrorism and Islam are Intimately Connected;" originally pub-lished in German as "Terrorismus und Islam hängen zusammen," in the *Frank-furter Allgemein,* 19 August 2017. Republished in English online at https://www.baytarrahmah.org/media/2017/FAZ_A-Conversation-with-Kyai-Haji-Yahya-Cholil-Staquf_08-19-17.pdf.

C. Holland Taylor, "Maneuver in the narrative space: Lessons from Islam Nusantara," *Strategic Review* 8:1 January – March 2018, pp. 36-51; https://www.baytarrah mah.org/media/2018/Strategic-Review_Maneuvering-within-Islam's-narrati ve-space_Jan-Mar-2018.pdf.

Yahya Cholil Staquf, "Enduring threat, global ramifications," *Strategic Review* 8:3, July – September 2018, pp. 12-17; https://www.baytarrahmah.org/media/2018/Strategic-Review_Enduring-threat_global-ramifications_Jul-Sep-2018.pdf.

Yahya Cholil Staquf, adopted by the National Conference of Nahdlatul Ulama Religious Scholars 1 March 2019, "The Recontextualization of *Fiqh* (Islamic Law) and Transformation of the Prevailing 'Muslim Mindset,' for the Sake of World Peace and to Achieve a Harmonious Communal Life for all Mankind." This document is also called informally "2019 Munas;" https://www.baytarrahmah.org/me dia/2019/2019-Munas_The-Recontextualization-of-Fiqh.pdf.

Yahya Cholil Staquf, "To prevent another Christchurch, Islam must confront the at-tacks in its name that have radicalised the West," *The Telegraph,* 24 March 2019; https://www.telegraph.co.uk/news/2019/03/24/prevent-another-christchur ch-islam-must-confront-attacks-name/.

Yahya Cholil Staquf, "Responding to a Fundamental Crisis Within Islam Itself," *Public Discourse: The Journal of the Witherspoon Institute*, 11 July 2020; https://www.the publicdiscourse.com/2020/07/64947/.

Background and context in chronological order:

Samuel P. Huntington, "The Clash of Civilizations?" *Foreign Affairs,* Vol. 72, No. 3, Summer, 1993, pp. 22-49.

Samuel P. Huntington, *The Clash of Civilizations and the Remaking of World Order* (New York: Simon & Schuster, 1996), 368 pp.

Mujiburrahman, "Islam and Politics in Indonesia: The Political Thought of Abdurrahman Wahid," *Islam and Christian—Muslim Relations*, Vol. 10, No. 3, 1999; pp. 339-352.

Bernard Lewis, *The Crisis of Islam: Holy War and Unholy Terror* (New York: Random House, 2003), 224 pp.

Robert W. Hefner, "Muslim Democrats and Islamist Violence in Post-Soeharto Indonesia," pp 273-301 in Robert W. Hefner, ed. *Remaking Muslim Politics: Pluralism, Contestation, Democratization,* Princeton Studies in Muslim Politics vol. 26 (Princeton University Press, 2004).

Paul Wolfowitz, "Wahid and the Voice of Moderate Islam," obituary for President Abdurrahman Wahid, *The Wall Street Journal*, 10 January 2010; https://www.wsj. com/articles/SB10001424052748704842604574642353284811682.

Hodri Ariev, "Islam: Torn between Blessing and Cursing," paper presented at Oceans of Revelations Screening as an introductory lecture on "Liberal Islam: Indonesian Islam—liberal influences from Southeast Asia," held by the Friederich Nourman Stiftung, 24 November 2010, Bucerius Law School, Hamburg, Germany; https://www.academia.edu/1325060/ISLAM_Torn_Between_Blessing_and_Cursing.

Paul Marshall and Nina Shea, *Silenced: How Apostasy and Blasphemy Codes are Choking Freedom Worldwide* (Oxford University Press, 2011), 480 pp.

Fernando Perez, "Why Religious Violence has Grown in Indonesia," World Evangelical Alliance, Religious Liberty Commission, 24 February 2011; https://www.gos pelherald.com/articles/47076/20110224/why-religious-violence-has-grown-in-indonesia.htm.

Ahmad al-Raysuni, *Imam Al-Shatibi's Theory of the Higher Objectives and Intents of Islamic Law,* original edition translated from Arabic by Nancy Roberts, abridged by Alison Lake (Herndon, VA, USA: International Institute of Islamic Thought, 2013).

Martin van Bruinessen, "Abdurrahman Wahid," *The Encyclopaedia of Islam*, Third Edition, 2013 Part 2013-1, pp. 4-9; https://www.academia.edu/3167991/Abdurrah man_Wahid?email_work_card=view-paper.

Alex P. Schmid, "Violent and Non-Violent Extremism: Two Sides of the Same Coin?" (The Hague: International Centre for Counter-Terrorism, 2014), 31 pp.

https://www.icct.nl/download/file/ICCT-Schmid-Violent-Non-Violent-Extre
mism-May-2014.pdf.

Joe Cochrane, "From Indonesia, a Muslim Challenge to the Ideology of the Islamic State," *The New York Times*, November 26, 2015; https://www.nytimes.com/ 2015/11/27/world/asia/indonesia-islam-nahdlatul-ulama.html.

R. Rania Shah, "Saint Thomas Aquinas and Imam Al-Ghazālī on the Attainment of Happiness," *The International Journal of Religion and Spirituality in Society* 6:2 (Champaign, Illinois, USA: Common Ground Publishing, 2015), 18 pp.

Jayson Casper, "The World's Biggest Muslim Organization Wants to Protect Christians," *Christianity Today*, 18 May 2016; https://www.christianitytoday.com/ news/2016/may/more-than-300-islamic-leaders-denounce-extremism.html.

Rüdiger Lohlker, "Theology Matters: The Case of Jihadi Islam," *Strategic Review* 6:3, July – August 2016, pp. 93 – 105; https://www.baytarrahmah.org/media/2016/Stra tegic-Review_Theology-matters-The-case-of-jihadi-Islam_Jul-Sep-2016_highli ghted.pdf.

Alex P. Schmid, "Moderate Muslims and Islamist Terrorism: Between Denial and Resistance" (The Hague: International Centre for Counter-Terrorism, 2017), 28 pp. https://icct.nl/publication/moderate-muslims-and-islamist-terrorism-betwe en-denial-and-resistance/.

Alexander R Arifianto, "Islam Nusantara & Its Critics: The Rise of NU's Young Clerics," *RSIS Commentary*, 23 January 2017; https://www.rsis.edu.sg/wp-content/up loads/2017/01/CO17018.pdf.

Krithika Varagur, "Indonesia's Moderate Islam is Slowly Crumbling: Liberal Muslims are fretting as fundamentalists seize the popular moment." *Foreign Policy*, 14 February 2017; https://foreignpolicy.com/2017/02/14/indonesias-moderate-islam-is-slowly-crumbling/.

Paul Marshall, "Indonesia's Blasphemy Conviction Threatens Muslim Democracy. But I Still Have Hope. Why Christians should support the type of Muslims who support Ahok." *Christianity Today*, 11 May 2017; https://www.christianitytoday. com/ct/2017/may-web-only/indonesia-blasphemy-threatens-muslim-democ racy-ahok-jakarta.html.

Kate Shellnutt, "Pence Meets Indonesia's Top Muslim Leader After Church Attacks," *Christianity Today*, 18 May 2018; https://www.christianitytoday.com/news/20 18/may/mike-pence-staquf-indonesia-church-attack-nahdlatul-ulama.html.

Paul Marshall, "Conflicts in Indonesian Islam," *Current Trends in Islamist Ideology*, Hudson Institute, 31 May 2018; https://www.hudson.org/research/14367-con flicts-in-indonesian-islam.

Yaakov Katz, "A Message of Peace and Rahma: The leader of the world's largest Islamic movement visits Jerusalem bringing a universal message of Islam," *Jerusalem Post*, 15 June 2018; https://www.jpost.com/opinion/editors-notes-a-message-of-peace-and-rahma-560062.

Paul Marshall, "Countering Extremism In Indonesia and Beyond," *Cornerstone* (RFI), 22 June 2018; https://www.religiousfreedominstitute.org/blog/countering-ex tremism-in-indonesia-and-beyond.

Muhammad Zuhdi, "Challenging Moderate Muslims: Indonesia's Muslim Schools in the Midst of Religious Conservatism," *Religions* 2018, 9(10), 310; https://www. mdpi.com/2077-1444/9/10/310.

Paul Marshall, "Blasphemy Returns as a Political Weapon in Indonesia," *Providence*, 31 October 2018; https://providencemag.com/2018/10/blasphemy-returns-polit ical-weapon-indonesia-jokowi/.

Bernard Adeney-Risakotta, *Living in a Sacred Cosmos: Indonesia and the Future of Islam* (Yale University, 2018), 426 pp.

Brian L Steed, "Maneuvering within Islam's narrative space," *Strategic Review* 8:1, Janu ary – March 2018, pp. 16-35; https://www.baytarrahmah.org/media/2018/Stra tegic-Review_Maneuvering-within-Islam's-narrative-space_Jan-Mar-2018.pdf.

Paul Marshall, "The Ambiguities of Religious Freedom in Indonesia," *The Review of Faith & International Affairs*, 16:1, March 2018, pp. 85-96; https://www.tandfonline.com/ doi/full/10.1080/15570274.2018.1433588.

Raymond Ibrahim, *Sword and Scimitar: Fourteen Centuries of War between Islam and the West* (Da Capo Press, 2018), 352 pp.

James M. Dorsey, "Reforming the Faith: Indonesia's Battle for the Soul of Islam," *Hori zons: Journal of International Relations and Sustainable Development,* Winter, 2019, pp. 150-171; https://www.cirsd.org/en/horizons/horizons-winter-2019-issue no-13/reforming-the-faith.

Paul Marshall, "Muslim Leader Yahya Cholil Staquf: Need to Address 'Problematic El ements of Islamic Orthodoxy' After Christchurch Attack," *Religion Unplugged*, April 3, 2019; https://religionunplugged.com/news/2019/4/3/muslim-leader yahya-cholil-staquf-need-to-address-problematic-elements-of-islamic-ortho doxy-after-christchurch-attack.

Benjamin Soloway, "What's at Stake in Indonesia's Elections?" *Foreign Policy*, April 16, 2019, 6 pp; https://foreignpolicy.com/2019/04/16/whats-at-stake-in-indone sias-elections/.

Paul Marshall, "Muslims and Evangelicals form Joint Working Group to Counter Ex tremism," *Providence*, 27 April 2020; https://providencemag.com/2020/04/ muslims-evangelicals-form-joint-working-group-counter-extremism/?fbclid= IwAR0vsxcXtwMWTKsCLIwQG8rB--5vXixR2OalZ57sChCJUFnouuMJ6x0BU1Q.

H. Muhaimin Iskandar, "The future of civilization: Indonesia's contribution," *Strategic Review*, 2 July 2020, pp. 1-5; https://www.baytarrahmah.org/media/2020/Stra tegic-Review_The-Future-of-Civilization_Indonesia%E2%80%99s-Contribution _07-02-20.pdf.

Timothy Shah and Thomas Dinham, "Humanitarian Islam: Fostering shared civiliza tional values to revitalize a rules-based international order," *Strategic Review,* 2 July 2020, pp. 7-18; https://www.baytarrahmah.org/media/2020/Strategic-

Review_Humanitarian-Islam_Fostering-Shared-Civilizational-Values_07-02-20.pdf.

James M. Dorsey, "Indonesia: A Major Prize in the Battle for the Soul of Islam," *Inside Arabia,* 30 July 2020; https://insidearabia.com/indonesia-a-major-prize-in-the-battle-for-the-soul-of-islam/.

Timothy Shah, ed., *Indonesia Religious Freedom Landscape Report 2020* (Religious Freedom Institute, 2020); https://www.baytarrahmah.org/media/2020/RFI_Indonesia+Landscape+Report+ONLINE.pdf.

Thomas K. Johnson, "A Case for Ethical Cooperation Between Evangelical Christians and Humanitarian Islam," *Evangelical Review of Theology* 44:3, August 2020, pp. 204-217;   https://theology.worldea.org/wp-content/uploads/2020/07/ERT-Vol-44-No-3-August-2020.pdf.

World Evangelical Alliance

World Evangelical Alliance is a global ministry working with local churches around the world to join in common concern to live and proclaim the Good News of Jesus in their communities. WEA is a network of churches in 129 nations that have each formed an evangelical alliance and over 100 international organizations joining together to give a worldwide identity, voice and platform to more than 600 million evangelical Christians. Seeking holiness, justice and renewal at every level of society – individual, family, community and culture, God is glorified and the nations of the earth are forever transformed.

Christians from ten countries met in London in 1846 for the purpose of launching, in their own words, "a new thing in church history, a definite organization for the expression of unity amongst Christian individuals belonging to different churches." This was the beginning of a vision that was fulfilled in 1951 when believers from 21 countries officially formed the World Evangelical Fellowship. Today, 150 years after the London gathering, WEA is a dynamic global structure for unity and action that embraces 600 million evangelicals in 129 countries. It is a unity based on the historic Christian faith expressed in the evangelical tradition. And it looks to the future with vision to accomplish God's purposes in discipling the nations for Jesus Christ.

Commissions:

- Theology
- Missions
- Religious Liberty
- Women's Concerns
- Youth
- Information Technology

Initiatives and Activities

- Ambassador for Human Rights
- Ambassador for Refugees
- Creation Care Task Force
- Global Generosity Network
- International Institute for Religious Freedom
- International Institute for Islamic Studies
- Leadership Institute
- Micah Challenge
- Global Human Trafficking Task Force
- Peace and Reconciliation Initiative
- UN-Team

Church Street Station
P.O. Box 3402
New York, NY 10008-3402
Phone +[1] 212 233 3046
Fax +[1] 646-957-9218
www.worldea.org

WEA
World Evangelical Alliance

Giving Hands

GIVING HANDS GERMANY (GH) was established in 1995 and is officially recognized as a nonprofit foreign aid organization. It is an international operating charity that – up to now – has been supporting projects in about 40 countries on four continents. In particular we care for orphans and street children. Our major focus is on Africa and Central America. GIVING HANDS always mainly provides assistance for self-help and furthers human rights thinking.

The charity itself is not bound to any church, but on the spot we are co-operating with churches of all denominations. Naturally we also cooperate with other charities as well as governmental organizations to provide assistance as effective as possible under the given circumstances.

The work of GIVING HANDS GERMANY is controlled by a supervisory board. Members of this board are Manfred Feldmann, Colonel V. Doner and Kathleen McCall. Dr. Christine Schirrmacher is registered as legal manager of GIVING HANDS at the local district court. The local office and work of the charity are coordinated by Rev. Horst J. Kreie as executive manager. Dr. theol. Thomas Schirrmacher serves as a special consultant for all projects.

Thanks to our international contacts companies and organizations from many countries time and again provide containers with gifts in kind which we send to the different destinations where these goods help to satisfy elementary needs. This statutory purpose is put into practice by granting nutrition, clothing, education, construction and maintenance of training centers at home and abroad, construction of wells and operation of water treatment systems, guidance for self-help and transportation of goods and gifts to areas and countries where needy people live.

GIVING HANDS has a publishing arm under the leadership of Titus Vogt, that publishes human rights and other books in English, Spanish, Swahili and other languages.

These aims are aspired to the glory of the Lord according to the basic Christian principles put down in the Holy Bible.

Baumschulallee 3a • D-53115 Bonn • Germany
Phone: +49 / 228 / 695531 • Fax +49 / 228 / 695532
www.gebende-haende.de • info@gebende-haende.de

Martin Bucer Seminary

Faithful to biblical truth
Cooperating with the Evangelical Alliance
Reformed

Solid training for the Kingdom of God
- Alternative theological education
- Study while serving a church or working another job
- Enables students to remain in their own churches
- Encourages independent thinking
- Learning from the growth of the universal church.

Academic
- For the Bachelor's degree: 180 Bologna-Credits
- For the Master's degree: 120 additional Credits
- Both old and new teaching methods: All day seminars, independent study, term papers, etc.

Our Orientation:
- Complete trust in the reliability of the Bible
- Building on reformation theology
- Based on the confession of the German Evangelical Alliance
- Open for innovations in the Kingdom of God

Our Emphasis:
- The Bible
- Ethics and Basic Theology
- Missions
- The Church

Our Style:
- Innovative
- Relevant to society
- International
- Research oriented
- Interdisciplinary

Structure
- 15 study centers in 7 countries with local partners
- 5 research institutes
- President: Prof. Dr. Thomas Schirrmacher
  Vice President: Prof. Dr. Thomas K. Johnson
- Deans: Thomas Kinker, Th.D.;
  Titus Vogt, lic. theol., Carsten Friedrich, M.Th.

Missions through research
- Institute for Religious Freedom
- Institute for Islamic Studies
- Institute for Life and Family Studies
- Institute for Crisis, Dying, and Grief Counseling
- Institute for Pastoral Care

www.bucer.eu • info@bucer.eu
Berlin | Bielefeld | Bonn | Chemnitz | Hamburg | Munich | Pforzheim
Innsbruck | Istanbul | Izmir | Linz | Prague | São Paulo | Tirana | Zurich